THE SPIRAL OF TIME SERIES

RAV DOVBER PINSON

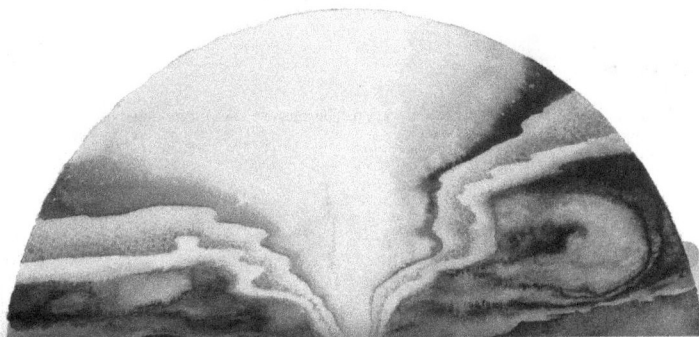

THE MONTH *of* SIVAN

vol 4

◆•THE ART OF RECEIVING•◆
SHAVUOS & MATAN TORAH

IYYUN
PUBLISHING

IYYUN PUBLISHING

Published by IYYUN Publishing
232 Bergen Street
Brooklyn, NY 11217

http:/www.iyyun.com

Iyyun Publishing books may be purchased for educational, business or sales promotional use. For information please contact: contact@IYYUN.com

Editor: Reb Matisyahu Brown

Developmental Editor: Reb Eden Pearlstein

Proofreading / Editing: Simcha Finkelstein

Cover and book design: RP Design and Development

Cover image:
"Sivan" by Federico Parolo from The Misaviv Hebrew Circle Calendar by Deuteronomy Press.
www.circlecalendar.com

pb ISBN 978-1-7338130-5-1

Pinson, DovBer 1971-
The Month of Sivan: The Art of Receiving
1.Judaism 2. Jewish Spirituality 3. General Spirituality

vol **4**

THE MONTH
of SIVAN

◆• THE ART OF RECEIVING •◆
SHAVUOS & MATAN TORAH

IYYUN PUBLISHING

ב״ה

CONTENTS

2 | OPENING

5 | THE MONTH OF SIVAN: An Overview

12 | PERMUTATION OF HASHEM'S NAME

14 | TORAH VERSE

16 | LETTER

20 | NAME OF THE MONTH

22 | SENSE

23 | SIGN

27 | TRIBE

29 | BODY PART

32 | ELEMENT

34 | TORAH PORTIONS

36 | SEASON OF THE YEAR

39 | THE HOLIDAY OF THE MONTH

85 | SUMMARY OF ADAR

88 | PRACTICE & INTENTION

CONTENTS
PART TWO: ESSAYS ON SHAVUOS & MATAN TORAH

94 | FIFTY DAYS FROM SHABBOS OR FROM PESACH:
Receiving or Participating with Time & Torah

112 | WHEN AND WHERE WAS THE TORAH GIVEN

118 | THE NIGHT OF MATAN TORAH:
From Klal to Prat and back to Klal

130 | THE ESSENCE OF SHAVUOS:
The Keser of Torah

167 | THE 50TH LEVEL:
Beyond the Possibility of Ra / Negativity & Sin

182 | MATAN TORAH / THE DAY THE TORAH WAS GIVEN:
Receiving the Torah Everyday Anew

188 | CONNECTING TO THE WHITE & BLACK FIRES OF
THE TORAH & THEIR UNITY

207 | SHAVUOS: Beyond all Avodah

211 | THE EVOLUTION OF KLAL YISRAEL:
From Am / People, to Eidah / Congregation, to Goy
Echad / One Nation

~ϙ~

OPENING

*E*ACH MONTH OF THE YEAR RADIATES WITH A DISTINCT quality and provides unique opportunities for personal growth and spiritual illumination. Accordingly, every month has a slightly different climate and represents a particular stage in the 'story of the year' as expressed through the annual cycles of nature. The winter months call for practices and pursuits that are intrinsically different than those of the summer months. Some months are filled with holidays, some have only one, and others none. Each month therefore has its own natural and spiritual 'signature.'

According to the deeper levels of Torah, each month's distinct qualities, opportunities, and natural phenomena correspond to a twelve-part symbolic structure. The spiritual nature of each month is articulated in 12 points of light: 1) a permutation of Hashem's

Four-Letter name 2) a verse from the Torah 3) a letter of the Aleph Beis 4) the meaning of the month's name 5) an experiential "sense" 6) a Zodiac sign 7) a tribe of Israel 8) a body part 9) a natural element 10) a unit of successive Torah portions that are read during the month 11) a season of the year 12) the holidays that occur during the month.

By reflecting on these twelve aspects, an ever-ascending spiral of insight, understanding, and practical action is revealed. Learning to navigate and harness the nature of change, by holistically engaging with the cycles of time, adds a deeper sense of purpose and heightened presence to our lives.

In this present volume we will delve into the spiritual nature of the month of Sivan according to these twelve categories.

❦

NOTE: *For a more comprehensive treatment of this twelve-part system and the overarching dynamics of the "story of the year," an in-depth introduction has been provided in Volume One of this series,* The Spiral of Time: Unraveling the Yearly Cycle.

ɣ

The Month of Sivan:

The Art of Receiving.
Shavuos & Matan Torah

S PRING IS A MONTH OF RENEWAL. After a long, cold and dark winter the weather is finally turning, the flowers are budding, the birds are chirping, the grass is starting to grow. The whole world around us begins to feel more alive, vibrant and invigorated.

We, who are also a part of the biosphere, respond in kind — we mirror this sense of renewal. Spring comes along and we begin to feel full of aliveness. We are naturally pulled in numerous exciting directions, whether towards new adventures, opportunities, or relationships.

The first month of the spring is Nisan, the month of the historical Exodus from Egypt, and a time in which we inwardly leave our own enslavements and claim our own freedom, openness and aliveness. When Nisan takes hold, we move out of our 'winter hibernation.' This seasonal and spiritual transition is celebrated on *Pe-*

sach / Passover and symbolizes the Exodus from everything which exile represents: alienation, separation, lack of clarity, doubt, and the sense of being lost. In our experience of the warming weather, we sense freedom in the air, not just as a budding potential, but as a vivid blossoming reality.

Then comes the second month, Iyyar. Following our miraculous birth into freedom and vitality, we begin to feel more self-assured and expressive. Iyyar is thus the month of individuality. We also count each individual day of the month, as it is entirely encompassed within the period of *Sefira* / counting of the days leading into the Festival of Shavuos. Iyyar is the month and Mazal of the Bull, which is an aggressive quality. As we begin to find our individual voice we can become aggressive and loud, even to the point of lacking *Kavod* / honor for others. During Iyyar the students of the First Century sage Rebbe Akiva died mostly during the month of Iyyar, "because they did not respect each other," as explored in the book, *The Month of Iyyar: Evolving the Self & Lag B'Omer.*

Then comes Sivan, the third month of the year and of spring. When Sivan comes along everything seems to settle down and find balance; after the excitement and newness of Nisan and the aggressive individuality of Iyyar. The number three symbolizes harmony and equilibrium. Thus we experience a *Hisyashvus* / settling down; we begin to feel more comfortable in our skin.

The first month is associated with Avraham and the emotional attribute of *Chesed* / kindness and giving; our liberation from Egypt during this month is a gift from Above. The second month is associated with Yitzchak and the attribute of *Gevurah* / strength, separation, and thus longing. The third month, Sivan, is associated with the attribute of *Tiferes* / beauty, harmony, and integration, and with Ya'akov, one of the *twin* brothers (*Pesikta Rabsi*, Parsha 28:5). Ya'akov is the 'perfect' Patriarch, the integration of Avraham's love and Yitzchak's strength. Tiferes, like the third element in any sequence or series, is a dimension of unification.

The first element in a series signifies the oneness that excludes and rules out any multiplicity, free of all limitations and duality. This is the quality of breaking free from the limitations and dualistic or idolatrous spirituality of *Mitzrayim* / Egypt. The name *Mitzrayim* itself comes from the root word *Metzar* / constriction or limitation.

The second element of a series signifies two-ness, duality, multiplicity and separation. It is often experienced as a longing to create unity. This is the quality of the month of Iyyar. An exaggerated expression of this kind of 'two-ness' is the 'terrible-twos' of young children. In this toddler stage they begin to find their voice and their fledgling instinctual need for independence. Suddenly everything is, "Mine! Mine!" and "Now! Now!" This swing into individuality can lead to an exclusion of the needs and *Kavod* / honor/respect of others, perhaps even for someone's own mother.

During the Exodus from Egypt we were born spiritually, and were in a state of 'infancy' during the latter part of Nisan. With the month of Iyyar we begin to enter a new phase of inner development, one in which we start to express our sense of separate selfhood. Our Sages draw a parallel between an infant and the Mazal/zodiac sign of Nisan, *Taleh* / Aries / the Lamb. When a tender, meek, lamb-like infant grows a little older and stronger it becomes more like an aggressive *Shor* / taurus / young bull, the sign of Iyyar (*Tanchumah*, Ha'azinu). We do need to affirm ourselves and become individuals, but in a way that is healthy and respectful of ourselves as well as others. This leads us to the third stage of our spiritual development.

A third element in a series signifies a unity that synthesizes both the absolute oneness of the first element and the multiplicity of the second. This is unity without an opposite, a singularity that embraces and includes multiplicity without its unity being altered.

Nisan is the *Klal* / whole, the unity that precedes the individuality. Iyyar is all about the *Prat* / distinct individual aspects. Sivan is about the Klal that comes after and includes the Prat (Chidushei Harim, *Sefer HaZechus*, Sefirah/Chodesh Iyyar). The Shor, the Mazal of Iyyar, is an aggressive animal and represents strong individuality, thus even its horns are "comprised of individual layers" (*Rosh Hashanah*, 26a). Sivan's Mazal of *T'umim* / twins, as will be explored, represents a unity of two in the larger context of a unit (*Shem miShemuel*, Shemini, 5672. Kedoshim, 5673).

In the diagram of *Sefiros* / Divine attributes, Tiferes rests in between Chesed and Gevurah; it unites and integrates these opposites. Chesed is limitless giving, and Gevurah is total restriction and retention. Chesed is about the giver and the need to give. Gevurah is about the receiver. Tiferes is the balanced emotion of compassion in which one gives, not out of a selfish need to give, but rather out of compassion for the receiver. In this mode one might also receive, but not out of selfishness or aggression, rather out of a sensitive awareness of the giver.

This third month of the year is thus a month of connection and unification. It is a month that draws together Chesed or Divine giving, and Gevurah or human receiving. It draws together the opposites of Heaven and earth, physical and spiritual, body and soul. Sivan is when the ultimate unifier, the Torah, was given. The word *Tiferes*, our Sages say (Berachos, 58a. *Tikunei Zohar*, Tikun 21), refers to the Giving of the Torah. Tiferes is in the middle column of the diagram of Sefiros, which balances and unifies the right and left columns, masculine and feminine.

Torah is an expression of the essential *third*. A certain Galilean lectured before Rav Chisda, "Blessed is Hashem who gave the three-part Torah (Torah, Prophets and Holy Writings) to the three-fold nation (Kohen, Levi and Yisrael), by means of a third-born: Moshe (who followed Aaron and Miriam in birth order), on the third day (of the separation of men and women), in the third month (Sivan)" / בריך רחמנא דיהב אוריאן תליתאי לעם תליתאי עַל יְדֵי תליתאי ביום תליתאי בירחא תליתאי (Shabbos, 88a). In addition, the Torah was given to the people who descended from the three *Avos* / Patriarchs Avraham, Yitzchak and Ya'akov. It was given by Moshe who was a descendant of the third tribe, Levi. In Hebrew, the name *Moshe* has three letters and *Levi* also has three letters (Rabbeinu Nisim Gaon, *ad loc*).

"The day of *Matan Torah* / the giving of the Torah was like a great wedding" (Ta'anis, 26b), uniting all aspects of Divinity and humanity.

King Shlomo / Solomon says, "Your bosoms are like two fawns, the twins of a gazelle, who graze among the roses" (Shir haShirim, 4:5). The "right hand" is an embodiment of *Chesed* / giving, while the left hand is an embodiment of *Gevurah* / restriction. Between the two arms lies the bosom, as the Zohar says, which represents the middle column connecting the two. The Torah is what lies between the left and right, unifying the opposites. In the month of the Gemini / twins, we received the two *Luchos* / Tablets, which revealed the principle of the *third*, the Torah of unification.

There are two different kinds of *thirds*. The middle-column Sefirah of Tiferes is mapped as a unifying 'third' beneath Chesed and Gevurah. The highest Sefirah, the aspect of *Keser* / Crown is a 'third' that is above and beyond the polarities of Sefiros, columns, and dualities. Experientially, Keser is manifest as transcendental will and desire. The Torah is associated with the lower unification of Tiferes, but it is rooted in the transcendent reality of Keser which unifies polarities by being beyond them.

As we will soon explore in greater detail, Torah is deeply associated with Keser. Our Sages speak of the "crown of Torah" (*Avos*, 4:17), and teach that at Mount Sinai we all received two 'crowns' (*Shabbos*, 88a). Today, the 'crown of Torah' is available and accessible to all, "[It is] in its place. All who want to take it, let him come and take" (*Yuma*, 72b).

In the Oral Torah, Gemara and Medrash, we frequently read accounts such as, "A certain Galilean lectured before Rav Chisda." Why is it important to record who delivered the teaching and to whom? It is because a dialogue between two reveals a hidden third; when one individual speaks to another, the third element present is the idea itself. This is the element that unites the speaker and the listener.

The above account is especially expressive of this principle. Rav Chisda, as his name suggests, is connected to the attribute of Chesed. The Galilean is related to Gevurah. One of the reasons that the teachings of the Galileans were not protected is that they did not share their teachings with others (*Eiruvin*, 53. Rashi, first under-standing); they withheld their Torah, in the mode of Gevurah. Here, however, the Galilean is sharing his Torah, and there is a revealing of the third unifying component. By communicating Torah with another, he reveals that the entire Torah is about the construct of *three*.

Keser is the unity of the opposites of oneness and two-ness. 'One' means a singularity, a unity prior to diversification. There is only infinite Oneness in this level; unity to the exclusion of any-thing else. 'Two' represents separation, division and finitude. The world of 'two-ness' is expressed in the second day of Creation, in which the separation between the upper and lower waters occurs. In two-ness, multiplicity, the paradigm of oneness appears to be entirely absent. *Three*, however, comes after one and two, and thus contains both. 'Three' represents a unity that paradoxically contains both the static singularity of *one*, and the deep separation of *two*. This is the paradox of Existence itself; it is the Divine Oneness that transcends the apparent world of duality while simultaneously embracing it and constituting it. This is the essential unity that includes both infinitude and finitude.

☾

ᎧᏙ

PERMUTATION OF HASHEM'S NAME

*T*HE MOST ESSENTIAL NAME OF THE DIVINE SOURCE OF Reality is the Name "Hashem," the four letter Name, Yud-Hei-Vav-Hei. A rearrangement of these four letters produces the word *HaVaYaH*, which means *Haviyah* / bringing being into being. This is understood as referring to the Ultimate Being, which is both the Source *and* Substance of all being. The Ultimate Being does not depend on anything else to exist. It gives rise to all past, present and future manifestations, thereby bringing all things into existence 'ex nihilo' or *Yesh meAyin* / being from non-being.

A linguistic interpretation of the four letters composing the Name in its regular sequence is important to understand. The last three letters of the Name, Hei-Vav-Hei, create the word *Hoveh /* is – the present. The root of this verb means *to bring into being.* The first letter of the Name, Yud, serves as a prefix to the last three letters, *Hoveh*, which modifies the verb to indicate a perpetual activity. In other words, the Name can mean, 'That Which is Continuously Bringing Created Being into Being.'

Hashem is the Source of time and is thus connected to actual time and all its subdivisions. In these volumes the focus is on how the four letters of the Name are articulated and permutated to express the inner light of each month of the year. Each letter permutation communicates a different spiritual dynamic encoded within the Divine signature of a particular month. The letter-sequence of Hashem's name connected with the month of Sivan is Yud-Vav-Hei-Hei.* In this sequence, the masculine letters Yud (י) and Vav (ו) are on one side and the feminine letters, Hei and Hei (ה) are on the other. These two opposite energies face each other like marriage partners, or like a male twin opposite a female twin. This letter-sequence thus alludes to the astrological sign of Sivan, Gemini or twins. Even though they are opposites, they also form one Name, thus they represent the unification of Heaven and Earth, the spiritual and the physical, the soul and body. This balance and unity between polarities in the 'third month' is an expression of *three,* as above.

☾

---

* The vowels in the sequence of Hashem's name for the month of Sivan are Sh'va-Yud, Kubutz-Vav, Patach-Hei, and Patach-Hei.

༄

TORAH VERSE

*T*HERE IS A TORAH VERSE ASSOCIATED WITH EACH MONTH that is connected to its unique Divine signature. The order of the letters in the Divine name for each month provides an acronym for each month's particular verse.

The Torah verse containing an acronym for the above letter-combination is from the Book of Shemos, chapter 26 spanning verses 19 and 20: "...*Ydosav. U-l'Tzela Ha-Mishkan Ha-Sheinis...*" / ... ‏ידתיו. ולצלע המשכן השנית‎... This translates as, "...tenons (connecting joints). And the second wall of the *Mishkan* / Tabernacle..."

‏צלע‎ / *Tzela*, the Hebrew word for "wall," comes from the word ‏צל‎ / *Tzeil* / shadow. A person's shadow is like their 'double' or twin. *Tzeil* can also refer to a person's spiritual body which can be compared to a mirror image of the physical body, a luminous shadow of sorts. Every human being possesses this type of Tzeil, also translated as "aura" or "ethereal body" (*Zohar* 1, p. 217b, 220a. *Ramban* and *Rabbeinu Bachya*, Bamidbar, 14:9. *Sefer Chassidim,* 547. *Sefer haEmunos,* 6:4). The Tzeil is not just a distilled transparent version of the physical body, it is the body's prototype; the prefiguration that existed as a primordial form prior to the birth of the physical body. Our relationship with this angelic-like double, so to speak, is symbiotic and reciprocal. It is the means through which the body expands and develops (*Sefer haEmunos,* 6:4). Conversely, it is sustained and cultivated by the person's behavior and mindset (*Beis Elokim,* Sha'ar haYesodos, 53). Our 'aura' is enlivened by the energies of our thoughts, words and actions.

Every dimension of being has two basic levels, body and soul; also known as vessel and light. And even within the vessel of the physical body there is a denser level, that of the flesh and the bones, and a more 'spiritual' level, the ethereal Tzeil. This month enables us to harmonize all the levels of our being. On personal as well as cosmic scales, the giving of the Torah harmonizes Heaven and earth.

In the verse of the month, the word *Shenis* in "...and the second..." alludes to the theme of two opposites that are nonetheless joined as one. This is the theme of the Mishkan and the Beis haMikdash, the physical space where the spiritual and physical worlds meet and mingle, where Transcendence is felt as Immanence; where one's soul and body are perfectly harmonized.

ז

LETTER

HERE ARE 22 LETTERS IN THE ALEPH BEIS. Three are called the Mother Letters, they are Aleph, Mem and Shin. Then there are seven letters that have both a harsh and soft pronunciation, as in, Beis (harsh) and Veis (soft). Finally there are twelve Simple Letters. The twelve 'simple' letters in the Aleph Beis are letters that do not have a harsh and soft pronunciation, and every month is connected with another one of these twelve letters. The letter of Sivan is Zayin (ז), the seventh letter of the Aleph-Beis. The Hebrew word for a seven-day week is שבוע / *Shavua* from the word שבע / *Sheva* / seven. In Sivan we complete the seven weeks of counting the Omer, the time period between Pesach and the holiday of *Shavuos*, which literally means, the Festival of Weeks.

Seven weeks following our Exodus from Egypt, we stood at the foot of Mount Sinai and received the Torah. The day of receiving the Torah was also on Shabbos, the seventh day of the week: דכולי עלמא בשבת ניתנה תורה לישראל / "Everyone agrees that on Shabbos the Torah was given to Israel" (*Shabbos*, 86b).

In addition to the association of Shabbos with seven (Zayin), Shabbos is also symbolic of the unity and harmony of Sivan. The holy rest of Shabbos *completes* our work-week efforts; the *holy* completes the *mundane*, and together these dimensions are called a week. On Shabbos, our soul fills our body, spirituality elevates our physicality, and these opposites become joined as one unit.

Graphically speaking, the letter Zayin is a gentle back-and-forth movement (ז) suggestive of the shifts of weight in walking. The small wave at the top of the letter moves, so-to-speak, to unify with the lower vertical wave, while the lower wave moves to unify with the higher wave. This symbolizes the spiritual quality of this month which allows us to 'walk' in *Olam haZeh* / this world, while remaining one with our higher spiritual identity; to strive for achievement in our lives and yet to be at peace at the same time.

Zayin can be seen as the Divine attribute of Tiferes, since when we count down from Keser, the seventh Sefirah is Tiferes* (*Zohar 3*,

---

* There are Ten *Sefiros* / Divine attributes. The first Sefirah is *Keser* / Crown. The quality of Keser is the deep desire and primordial will of the Infinite One to create finite existence. Keser is in the middle column. Next is *Chochmah* / wisdom and intuition (right column), then *Binah* / understanding and reason (left column), and then *Da'as* / practical knowledge (middle column). Next are the three primary emotions: Chesed, Gevurah and Tiferes. *Chesed* / kindness is giving and love (right column), *Gevurah* / strength is restriction or withholding (left column). Between Chesed and Gevurah there is their middle-col-

Parshas Emor, p. 102b). As mentioned, Tiferes is intimately connected with this third month and the giving of the Torah.

Normally, we would consider the seventh Sefirah to be Malchus (as it is the seventh of the emotional Sefiros) and thus the letter Zayin also represents Malchus. Malchus is the lowest of the ten Sefiros, and relates to this physical world. Like Tiferes, Malchus is a central/middle column Sefirah and is a unifier of opposites, as it receives and integrates all of the Sefiros above it and transmits their energy to the subsequent structure of Sefiros below it. This is a graphical representation of the fact that once we experience the higher 'rest' of Shabbos, we should bring that holiness down into the actions of the subsequent work-week.

The letter Zayin also looks like a battle-axe or a sword with a decorative hilt. The word *Zayyin,* in fact, means 'weapon' (*Pardes Rimonim,* Sha'ar haOsyos, 10). This reminds us that sometimes we must wage spiritual battles in order to elevate ourselves; no matter what happens, we must persevere and 'walk' forward in our lives. The numerical value of the word *Zayyin* is 77 (Zayin/7, Yud/10, Yud/10, Nun/50). This is also the value of the word *Oz* / strength (Ayin/70,

---

umn synthesis, *Tiferes* / harmony and compassion. Next are the three 'outer' emotions, Netzach, Hod and Yesod. *Netzach* / victory is confident ambition and empowerment (right column), *Hod* / devotion is humility (left column), *Yesod* / foundation is intimacy or relationship (middle column). And finally, *Malchus* / kingship or nobility is the aspect of receptivity (also, middle column). The Ten Sefiros are like ten screens through which the Infinite Light of the Creator penetrates our finite reality. The distinct forms, shapes and colors of the Sefiros filter the infinite colorless, formless, unified Light as it enters our world of form.

Zayin/7). In order to do battle we need *Oz*. The Zohar says that *Oz* refers to the Sefirah of Malchus (*Zohar* 3, p. 262b).

As we will soon explore, this month is connected with the sense of movement or walking. This sense implies 'marching' or relentlessly advancing forward in battle. And yet, the sense of movement in this month includes a feeling of *Savu'ah* / satisfaction. Being that our life's purpose is revealed to us during this month, with our reception of the Torah, there is a sense of 'rest' and stillness even in our marching forward. When the 'day of Shabbos' permeates our work and weekdays, we can then work hard, strive, aspire and walk steadily all the while without any anxiety or nervousness. Rather, our movement comes from, and expresses, a calm joy, openness and balance of *Tiferes* / harmony and beauty.

♈

NAME

ACH MONTH OF THE TWELVE MONTHS OF THE YEAR HAS A distinct name, and every name has a meaning. According to our Sages, the current names we have for the months were imported to our tradition upon our return to Israel from the Babylonian Exile. They can in fact be traced to ancient Babylonian or Akkadian names (*Yerushalmi*, Rosh Hashanah, 1:2, *Medrash Rabbah*, Bereishis, 48:9). In the times before the Babylonian Exile, the names of the months were mostly known by their number in the sequence of the year. For example, the month of Av was called the Fifth Month, and Cheshvan was known as the Eighth Month.

Before the Babylonian Exile, and in the Torah, Sivan is simply called the Third Month, with no particular name. After the Babylonian Exile, it is called Sivan. This name may come from the Akkadian word *Simanu* / appoint, which we can relate to the fact that this is the 'appointed' month for the giving and receiving of the Torah.

Sivan has four letters: Samach, Yud, Vav, and Nun. The last three of these letters spell יון / *YaVaN* / Greek. Graphically, these three letters descend lower and lower, from Yud י to Vav ו to a Final Nun ן. *Yavan* thus represents a descent with no end, like quick sand, a force that can pull a person lower and lower. However, the first letter in Sivan, *Samach*, as a word means *Somech* / assisting or supporting, and it thus represents the concept of *Semicha* / support (*Berachos*, 4b. *Zohar* 1, p. 3a. *Osyos d'Rebbe Akiva*, Samach). This means that when we allow Hashem to support us fully, even when we need to 'descend' into the world of work, we can yet remain pure and detached from it. In the words of the Rebbe of Kotzk, "If you truly want to be within this world, you need to stand above it." When we do so, Hashem holds us and prevents us from becoming *Nofel* / fallen (the Nun). When we are connected above to the Ultimate Transcendent One, we can appear to be falling but we will never fall low. This 'falling while not falling' is the idea of Tiferes and the inclusion of opposites, like the circular letter Samach (ס) which completely surrounds and 'includes' its inner space.

The letters Samach and Tzadik are interchangeable, since they are both dental consonants, meaning that we use the same part of the mouth to create both sounds. With a Tzadik instead of Samach, the word *Sivan* can be read as *Tziyon* / Zion, referring to the *Beis haMikdash* / the Holy Temple in Jerusalem, where the Divine Presence rested. A *Tzadik* / illumined righteous person, is one who can descend into the world, and yet remain calmly attached above to the Divine Presence.

SENSE

*S*EFER *YETZIRAH* SAYS THE 'SENSE' OR ACTIVITY OF THIS month is walking. This is the idea of orderly movement, as opposed to 'leaping' or transcending, which is the sense of the month of Nisan. In Sivan we move with the steadiness and composure of spiritual maturity, like the orderly travels of Israel in the desert. It is a time to own our clarity, insight, and understanding of life's purpose. We can now translate higher clarity into action, and take proactive steps in our spiritual progress. We can now stride into the world, illumined by the Torah, to bring light to all of Hashem's creatures.

♊
SIGN

T'ᴜᴍɪᴍ / ᴛᴡɪɴs ᴏʀ Gᴇᴍɪɴɪ, ɪs ᴛʜᴇ Mᴀᴢᴀʟ/ᴀsᴛʀᴏʟᴏɢɪ-
ᴄᴀʟ sign of Sivan (See also Rashi, *Baba Metziya*, 106b) *The Zohar*
(Yisro) notes that the Torah was given to the offspring of
Ya'akov, who was a twin, in the month of twins.

Nisan, the First Month, is the Mazal of the lamb, alluding to
selfless submission. In that state of oneness there is no difference
between *you* and *me*. Iyyar, the Second Month, is the Mazal of the
Bull, alluding to self-confidence. In that state of duality we build
up our separate identities and differences, and there is a potential
for selfish conflict between *you* and *me*. Sivan is the month of true
peace. The Mazal of the twins alludes to the co-existence of self-
lessness and self. Thus, in Sivan we can unite at Mount Sinai, under
our different tribal banners, yet "like one person with one heart"

(*Rashi* on Shemos, 19:2). As individuals and subgroups we may be different, yet we can exist in complete harmony.

In Nisan, we offer the Paschal lamb, the *Korban Pesach* / Passover sacrifice, when the Temple Mount is fully under our sovereignty. A lamb is offered (the *Mazal* / zodiac sign of *T'leh* / lamb) because we were thrust from Egypt and given freedom as gifts from Above; we were meek and without personal expression. With the Exodus, redemption and birth of Klal Yisrael, we're like a newborn. One infant can look the same as any other infant, as their personality is not yet being expressed or developed. We are like a lamb, a 'sheep-ish' animal that does not openly express a personality or agenda.

After infancy comes an age when a child starts to express individuality and begins discovering everything about himself. Assertions such as, "It's *my* toy!" and "*I* want..." are frequently heard. In Iyyar we are entering our terrible-twos. During the month of Iyyar the 24,000 students of Rebbe Akiva passed away, and the meta-root of their death was that they did not show *Kavod* / honor or respect for each other — they saw each other as primarily separate. The Mazal of Iyyar is Taurus / the bull, which is the quality of self-assertion and aggression, the opposite of submission.

Iyyar is a month without holidays, as it is simply time to work on self-discovery, self-development and self-expression. After a child has developed beyond the stage in which everything is 'mine' and 'all about me,' he can begin to enter a level of maturity and responsibility in which he is learning to coexist and share with other people. This is the dawning of the month of Sivan.

In Sivan we reach the ability to have mature, mindful, sensitive relationships and to make space for others. The personality of the other person is valid and so is mine. This is the month of the Twins: you *and* me, beyond the levels of 'not me' and 'only me.' Our receiving of the Torah was like this mature acceptance of responsibility.

Torah is the Divine intelligence and blueprint of creation. To be able to receive Divine intelligence we needed to be intelligent beings. This quality of intelligence, as well as the capacity for abstract and deductive thinking, is a human attribute. Thus, the sign of Gemini is one of the only two distinctly 'human' signs. All other signs, with the exception of Virgo, are either animals or objects.

Geminis are generally intellectual people, and free spirits with a deep yearning to know everything. They tend to gather information of all kinds. This intellectual flexibility can manifest as a tendency to leap quickly from one topic to the next, and Geminis can dislike being contained orderly in their pursuits. A rectification of these tendencies is to practice 'walking' — delving steadily into a single subject and considering opposing viewpoints, until the depths and details of the subject are fully 'received.'

When the words of the Heavenly Torah are fully 'received' and inscribed in our hearts and intellects, we can activate a unification of Heaven and earth. The Medrash Rabbah hints at this unification with a metaphor: until the giving of the Torah on Mount Sinai, the people of Rome could not 'descend' to Assyria, nor could the people of Assyria 'ascend' to Rome. That is, until the giving of the Torah, the default mode of human consciousness was separation. It was assumed that the Transcendent realm could never 'descend' to the earthly realm, nor could earthly beings 'ascend'; these realms could not meet. At Mount Sinai, the limited human intellect was penetrated by the Divine Intellect. Sivan allows us to relive this cosmic unification of opposites.

We who received the 'twin' Luchos are able to navigate *Ohr v'Choshech* / light and darkness (See *Pesikta Rabsi*, Parsha 20:2. Matan Torah. Zerah Ephrayim, *ad loc*). The nation of *Ivrim* (the name that referred to Klal Yisrael when they're in a condition of slavery. *Rabbeinu Bachya*, Mishpatim) became the Nation of Yisrael. The word *Yisrael* equals 541, which is the same value as the words *Ohr* (207) plus *v'Choshech* (334). (*Ohr* = Aleph/1, Vav/6, Reish/200 = 207 *V'Choshech* = Vav/6, Ches/8, Shin/300, Chaf/20 = 334. 207, 334 = 541.) The purpose of Israel is to bring a unification between light and darkness, between the spiritual and the physical, between Above and below.

We fully became a nation, *Klal Yisrael*, at Matan Torah. It is the Torah that defines us as a nation: לפי שאומתינו בני ישראל אינה אומה אלא בתורותיה / "The Nation of Yisrael is only a *nation* with Torah" (*Emunos v'De'os*, Ma'amar 3:7). Torah gives us the ability to be truly *Yisrael*, the bridgers of the spiritual and physical, the light and apparent darkness.

TRIBE

ZEVULUN IS THE TRIBE OF SIVAN. Zevulun begins with the letter Zayin, the letter of the month. In fact, Zevulun is the only tribe among all twelve containing the letter Zayin. Zayin personifies Zevulun.

Zevulun is the prototypical businessman who travels out into the world, yet remains faithful to his inner life. As Ya'akov says, *S'mach Zevulun b'Tzeisecha* / "Rejoice, Zevulun, in your travels" (*Devarim*, 33:18). True 'rejoicing' is only possible with a deep connection to spirituality.

Zevulun represents movement and progress. Pushing out and joining the success in the material world with a spiritual purpose.

Zevulun is the 'twin' of the tribe of Yissachar (the tribe of the month of Iyyar), the one who sits and learns Torah. Even though their callings and personalities are opposites, they unite in mutual support, as Zevulun makes money to support the Torah-study of Yissachar (*Rashi*, Vayechi, 49:14). Zevulun is the embodiment of Olam Hazeh / this world. His name contains the word Zevel, literally meaning *garbage,* and alluding to the 'emptiness' of this world. Zevulun's inner state of emptiness or self-nullification allows him to go out into the world and elevate it.

Tiferes / harmony, unity, or bringing together is the quality of the month; and so this month we also have the opportunity to make a Tikun or rectification for Tiferes of *Kelipah* / negative Tiferes. Negative Tiferes is created when we attempt to include things in ourselves that we cannot elevate through inclusion. The Torah encourages us to elevate all of creation, however there are some activities and foods that the Torah asks us to exclude — in other words, we can only elevate these phenomena by refraining and staying away from them. When we make this Tikun, we can elevate creation like Zevulun, uniting Heaven and earth.

When Zevulun's mother, Leah, gives him his name, she alludes to a unification of opposites: "Now my husband will make his permanent residence with me..." (Bereishis, 30:20). In this verse, *Zevul* / residence, also refers to the Beis haMikdash, the place where Heaven and earth join. One epithet for the Beis haMikdash is *Zevul Beis Tifarteinu* / Residence-House of Our Tiferes (Zemiros Shabbos), our total integration.

ૐ

BODY PART

*W*HILE NISAN IS CONNECTED TO THE RIGHT LEG, SIVAN is the left leg. Together, these two legs allow us to walk. In Nisan we are *given* revelation. We did not work to achieve our freedom. In this paradigm we do not earn freedom; it is a free gift. The *Mochin d'Gadlus* / expanded consciousness, clarity and lucidity of mind that we receive on Pesach night is essentially beyond our own reach. This is the right leg, the symbol of *Chesed* / giving. This exists without any participation of the *Mekabel* / receiver.

With only one leg, a person can hop or skip. Pesach means to 'skip' or leap over — to transcend order. When we leave Egypt we skip, so-to-speak, on our right leg. We leap beyond our ego by refraining from eating *Chametz* / leavening — refraining from 'leavened' self-importance and ego.

After Nisan comes the month of Iyyar, a time of growth and reintroducing the qualities of ego in a balanced way. During Iyyar we gradually earn the right to revelation through disciplined effort. We begin to include aspects of the 'left leg' of Gevurah. Thus, we bring the Omer offering of barley, which is animal food (*Sotah*, 14a. Mishnah, *Pesachim*, 3b), alluding to the feeding or strengthening of our animal soul or ego (*Likutei Torah*, Emor, 35b). When Sivan arrives, we have gained full access to our left leg and are finally able to walk on both legs as fully mature people. We are now participants in revelation, since we have become worthy *receivers*.

On Shavuos, at the Giving of the Torah, the first revelation we receive is, *Anochi Hashem Elokechah* / "I am Hashem your G-d." 'Your G-d' means that every individual at Mount Sinai experiences Hashem on their own level of understanding; a child according to his level and an older person according to theirs (התינוקות לפי כחן...הבחורים לפי כחן... והזקנים לפי כחן *Yalkut Shimoni*, Yisro, Remez, 286). *Elokim* represents imminence, limitation and Gevurah. The Name Hashem represents G-d beyond our level and understanding, unlimited transcendence and Chesed. *Anochi* is the unification of these two opposites; the Divine 'I' transcends and includes all manifestations.

Ani / אני means *I*. *Anochi* / אנכי has the letters of *Ani* plus the letter Chaf / כ. Anochi is thus כ-אני / k'Ani / *like* Ani. Chaf stands for כתר / Keser / crown, the crown that sits above the Head of the King, as it were, yet, also encircles, embraces and envelops the Head.

The letter of the month of Nisan is Hei, a silent letter, denoting 'rest' (*Zohar* 3, Behar). Rest is the transcendence of action, as exemplified by Shabbos, which is 'above' the six weekdays of action. In the rush of leaving Egypt, we did not have time to act — a transcendent power took us out. Nisan is 'far above' our heads. In Iyyar, we work on our inner liberation. This is *below*, within us. When we finally reach Shavuos, we no longer need to transcend our situation, nor do we need to focus so intently on inner growth. We can now walk with the calm strength of free people. In Sivan, we have joined the 'above' of Nisan with the 'below' of Iyyar; both dimensions are fully accessible to us, like a crown that fits so well it feels like an extension of self.

Our right leg, or one leg as mentioned, is connected with skipping, leaping or running. This rapid 'movement' is connected with the sense of the month of Nisan, the sense of speech. "He who sends forth His utterance unto earth, His word arrives with alacrity" (*Tehilim*, 147:15). Perfected speech, such as Divine speech, arrives swiftly, with alacrity. That is, the words instantaneously affect reality. When we redeem the potential of our own speech and align with the Ultimate Speech, our words and speech take on this instantaneously creative power. In Sivan we are finally able to walk steadily with both legs; with strength, rootedness and the integration of the 'above' swiftness of Nisan together with the subtle thoughtful movements 'below' of Iyyar.

♊

ELEMENT

S IVAN CORRESPONDS TO THE ELEMENT OF WIND. In the month of Sivan we receive the Torah. Following the Exodus from Egypt, a freedom *from* exile, we begin the journey into a freedom *to;* to choose a new way of life, a Torah-il-lumined lifestyle.

Wind/air is the gift of flexibility, openness, and the ability not to be stuck in preconceived ideas. It is also reflected in the sign of Gemini, and as such, it is the appropriate month in which we received the Torah, past tense, and receive 'newness' *from* the Torah. All our wisdom, all our new Torah that we will learn and integrate into our lives is received, albeit in potential, on the day of Shavuos, the day of reliving the receiving of the Torah.

MATAN TORAH OF THE ENTIRE YEAR

On the festival of Matan Torah, all our *Chidushim* / new insights and *Seichel* / intelligence for the entire year are given in potential. That is, on Shavuos a person receives all of that year's understanding of Torah as a *Klal* / general 'download.' All the Chidushim encoded in this Klal are what he will reveal during the coming year, as the Sefas Emes writes (Shavuos, Tav/Reish/Lamed/Hei). Said another way, we each receive a hidden *Nevuah* / prophecy on Shavuos, which is the *Cheilek* / part of Torah wisdom that we will understand in the coming year, and throughout the year we reveal what we had received (*Derech haMelech*, Shavuos).

We receive not only the wisdom of Torah, specifically, but all of the *Seichel* / intelligence that we will need in order to serve Hashem throughout the coming year (*Me'or Einayim*, Miketz). In this way, Shavuos is the headquarters of intelligence, a time to draw down a new level of consciousness, a new *Partzuf* / Divine structure, which is the Klal that will fuel our spiritual work for the entire year. Through the course of the year we need to draw this consciousness down and unpack what we received.

TORAH PORTIONS

*T*HE TORAH PORTIONS READ THIS MONTH ARE USUALLY Bamidbar, Naso, Beha'alosecha, and Shelach.

Overall, these first portions, beginning with Bamidbar, speak of the Journey in the Desert, which is the idea of *movement*, progressing in the right direction, taking steps — even while in a barren desert. We have been empowered to continually progress forward in life, even when passing through a spiritual wasteland.

Bamidbar speaks of the encampment of the tribes of Israel, everyone having their own place within a unified nation. Even when the tribes traveled, they walked in an orderly fashion. This was a unification of physical movement and the ethereal stillness of the desert.

These portions are speaking about the journey of Klal Yisrael from Egypt to the Land of Israel, although, the actual journey ended up taking 40 years.

Beha'alosecha has the two verses of *Vayehi bi-N'so'a haAron* / "And so it was, when the Ark (of the Covenant) traveled…" According to our Sages (*Shabbos,* 116a), these two verses, which are bookended with two inverted letter Nuns, are considered a separate 'book' of the Torah. Since this very small 'book' splits the book of Bamidbar into three sections, we can count seven 'books' of the Torah instead of five. Seven is the value of Zayin, the letter of this month. Seven also alludes to the natural world of time through which we all journey.

The first verse of *Vayehi bi-N'so'a haAron* speaks about the orderly movement of the tribes as they walked through the desert: "And so it was, when the Ark (of the Covenant) traveled…"

The second verse, "Whenever it came to rest," speaks of the sublime stillness that would manifest when the Ark would *rest,* and the Presence of Oneness would dwell among the myriads of Israel. This again alludes to the Zayin, the Seventh Day, of rest. The first verse also speaks of *scattering enemies,* alluding to *Zayyin* / weapon. In a state of spiritual maturity, which is an integration of rest and movement, Shabbos and weekday, Chesed and Gevurah, the 'enemies' within us are scattered or elevated and unified within their source.

ᐅᐤᐤ
SEASON OF THE YEAR

*A*FTER A COLD WINTER, SPRING COMES AS AN UN-
EARNED gift from Above, an almost 'unexpected'
blessing. This is Nisan. When the warmth returns,
we come alive, like a new beginning is offered to us. There is a
visceral sensation of renewal which is a reflection of the metaphys-
ical truth that Hashem is granting us a new level of freedom and
Mochin d'Gadlus / expansive and lucid clarity of mind. When Iyyar
comes along, spring has already been unfolding for a while and we
start to take it for granted. We may even feel as if we 'deserve' the
Chesed of spring, and so a subtle arrogance sets in. Life no longer
seems so much like a gift.

This is the theme of the demise of the 24,000 students of Rebbe Akiva between Pesach and Shavuos — they took one another for granted and did not 'respect' what a Divine gift each person was. The Torah asks us on Pesach to offer lambs and sheep on the Temple Mount, since in Nisan we are 'meek like lambs' in the face of the great generosity descending upon us. Iyyar has no Torah-based holidays, nor even clear Rabbinic holidays, no times of great generosity descending from Above, so we must work on ourselves to merit elevation from below. This work is an expression of spiritual ego — it is easy to apply oneself to 'earning' a higher level of spiritual merit while disregarding the merits of others. In Iyyar, the 24,000 students felt they deserved their own achievements more than the others, and this spiritual arrogance undermined their efforts.

When Sivan arrives, the heat of the sun can sometimes become uncomfortable, and we no longer take for granted the clement weather of spring. Arrogance is thus diminished and balanced with gratitude. On Shavuos we offered loaves of leavened bread on the Altar, turning our spiritual 'elevation' and arrogance over to HaKadosh Baruch Hu / the Holy One.

In unison with these seasonal changes, in Nisan we are extricated from physical, mental and spiritual constriction and are gifted *Gadlus* / greatness, expansiveness and clarity. Then in the month of Iyyar we feel pangs of separation and the desire for something new, we yearn for something new. Through this yearning we enlarge our vessels; if we do not have *Teshukah* / deep desire, we will have a 'full cup' which cannot be filled.

To be filled we need to break open our vessel and enlarge it in order to receive more. Many times people yearn deeply for change, but they actually just want everything and everyone but themselves to change. They want their vessel to be as is while the world around them 'improves.' This never works. During Iyyar we must fix and enlarge our own vessel. Then, by Sivan, we will have a strong/open vessel to receive a new level of wisdom.

☾

HOLIDAY OF THE MONTH

"FOR EVERYTHING THERE IS AN APPOINTED TIME" (*Koheles*, 3:1). In other words, everything happens according to Divine timing (Rebbe RaYatz, *Sefer haMa'amorim*, tav/shin/aleph, p. 59). Our Sages tell us that when we left Egypt, it was the appointed time for such liberation. Hashem took us out of Egypt in a "*Kosher / perfect month*, not too hot a month and not too cold..." (Rashi, *Sotah*, 2a). This means not only that it occurred in the historically appropriate time, but also at the right time of year — the season best suited for this expression of Redemption. This is the same principle behind every Yom Tov; the narrative and observance of each celebration or fast reflects and refracts the light of the natural world through a spiritual lens.

Furthermore, in the months that contain a *Yom Tov* / holiday, that Yom Tov embodies and encapsulates the energy of the entire month in condensed form. In a month that does not have a major holiday, that absence is also an expression of the unique quality of the month.

Sivan is characterized by Shavuos. In the beginning of Sivan we are still striving, and inwardly journeying, counting down the days to Shavuos, until we finally reach the sixth day of Sivan (and in the Diaspora the seventh day as well).

The word *Shavuos* means *weeks*, as it was our yearning throughout the seven weeks of separation that carried us here to the foot of Mount Sinai. *Shavuos* also comes from the word *Savua* / satisfaction, the satisfaction of finally arriving at the sacred mountain. The Torah was given on Shabbos, the *Shevi'i* / seventh day, the day of Savua.

Regarding the holiday called Shavuos, the Torah (*Vayikra*, 23:15-17) only says, "And you shall count unto yourselves from after the day of rest (following the first day of Pesach), from the day that you brought the sheaf of the waving; seven weeks shall there be complete... Count 50 days and you shall present a new meal-offering unto Hashem.... You shall bring out of your dwellings two wave-loaves... they shall be baked with leaven, for *Bikurim* / first-fruits unto Hashem."

These words do not tell us a story of Matan Torah or give us any explanation as to why we celebrate this holiday. This is unlike the Torah's narrative of Pesach, the going out of Egypt, or Sukkos, when Hashem made us dwell in *Sukkos* / temporary shelters as we journeyed in the desert. What the Torah does tell us in the above verses is that there is a Mitzvah to bring "two loaves of leavened bread." This is in clear contrast to Pesach when we must refrain from all leavened bread. The verses also tell us that Shavuos is when we perform the Mitzvah of Bikurim, the offering of the new fruit.

Torah itself does not clearly explain that Shavuos is the time of the giving of the Torah. This will be explored in detail later on. In our liturgy, established by the Men of the Great Assembly, we call Shavuos the *Z'man Matan Torah* / Time of the Giving of the Torah, and on this day we specifically celebrate the revealing of the Ten Commandments at Mount Sinai. On this day Heaven and earth merged in a revealed way, and henceforth, with the power of the Torah, we have the ability to reveal Divinity within every aspect of creation.

THE REVELATION OF THE *KESER* / CROWN OF CREATION

When the Torah was given at Mount Sinai we each received two 'crowns' upon our heads, one corresponding to the declaration *Naaseh* / "We will perform (the Torah's actions)," and another corresponding to the declaration *v'Nishmah* / "and we will listen to (and understand the Torah's meanings)" (*Shabbos*, 88a). As mentioned, 'crown' in Hebrew is *Keser*. The word *Keser* in its numerical value is 620 (Chaf/20, Tav/400, Reish/200), and this is the exact number of letters in the Ten Commandments. These 620 letters in turn correspond to the 613 Mitzvos plus the Seven Rabbinical Mitzvos (*Baal haTurim*, Shemos, 20:14). The central theme of Shavuos is Keser.

Parenthetically, crowns are reserved for royalty. The crown of the Kingdom of David was only able to fit the heads of those who came from the House of David (*Avodah Zara*, 44a. See *Sanhedrin*, 21b, Rashi ad loc). King David, who is the epitome of *Malchus* / kingdom, the King of Israel par excellence, passed away on Shavuos (Yerushalmi, *Chagigah*, 2:3). Also, he passed away when he was 70 years old (*Medrash Rabbah*, Bereishis, Vayechi, 96:4), which is another reference to *Sheva* / seven and *Savua* / satisfaction *and* he passes away on Shabbos, the seventh day of the week (*Shabbos*, 30a).

What is a crown? And what does a crown represent in terms of its spiritual root? Keser is the attribute of Divine desire, which is the desire to create. Everything we create begins with a desire. In that desire we envision the end result. A person may desire to write a book or build a dream home. When the desire arises, they know, without all the specific details, what they want to achieve. They see in their mind's eye the final product. Only then comes the arduous process of working out the details, building the house brick by brick, or writing sentence by sentence, until the project reaches fruition. The envisioned goal is not manifest until the product is completed. The trick though, is to maintain the vision throughout the entire process and not lose focus nor veer off course, nor get lost in the 'trees' and forget about the 'forest.'

Keser is the vision that began the whole project of Creation. It is the raison d'etre of Creation, The *Nekudah* / entire 'point' of Creation.

There is a Keser of our own life as well as a Keser of all creation. Keser is the vision and desire for a given creation, in which the objective of that creation is revealed prior to its formation. Thus it is the 'space' in which the ultimate purpose and meaning of life is laid out. When you connect to your Keser you connect to your true purpose. Often we find that people run around, busying themselves with one thing after another, without ever finding any *Sipuk Nefesh* / spiritual satisfaction, and that is because their Keser, the 'big picture' (also called the 50ᵗʰ Gate, as will be explained), is not revealed to them.

When we receive the Torah at Mount Sinai, when we truly receive Torah-consciousness, we stop running about, journeying, and looking around. We have arrived. At Matan Torah the end goal of our existence and also the means to reach that goal is revealed to us. When we reach the end of the *Sheva* / seventh week, we attain *Shavuos* / the 50ᵗʰ day, we reach complete *Savua* / satisfaction.

To be satisfied with the revealing of the Keser knowledge of your purpose does not mean to stop growing and become stagnant or complacent. To be human is to desire, to always yearn and strive for more (*Medrash Rabbah*, Koheles, 3:10). "Mankind was created to toil" (*Iyov*, 5:7. *Sanhedrin*, 99b). It is imperative for human beings to work and grow continuously; we were created to toil for growth. Our source of fulfilment and שמחה *Simcha* / happiness is צמחה *Tz'mi-chah* / growth (the Sin / שׁ and Tzadik / צ are interchangeable letters). Despite the discomforts of growing, we are designed to attain happiness and satisfaction through working on ourselves.

When the Keser of our personal lives is revealed to us, we then have enjoyment and a sense of ease even when toiling. When we understand why we are here, why our souls have come down to this world, what specifically we are meant to accomplish and how, then we meet life from a place of wholeness and satisfaction. "A Tzadik eats to satisfy his soul" (*Mishlei*, 13:25). The Zohar says this means that the Tzadik eats *from a place of* satisfaction (*Zohar 2*, Beshalach, 62b). 'Eating' implies need and a lack of wholeness and satisfaction; one is striving to fill their hungry stomach. A Tzadik, however, eats not to gain satisfaction, but is already whole.

This prior 'fullness' is the result of living from a place of Keser.

Keser is a *Makif* / surrounding light, like a crown sitting above the head, embracing, unifying and reconciling all the paradoxes of existence below. This embrace and reconciliation of paradoxes is reflected in the unique quality of Sivan. On the one hand its energy is one of *Savua* / restful satisfaction, but on the other hand it is one of movement. The body part of the month is the left leg, suggesting movement, the tribe of the month is Zevulun, a tribe of merchants who traveled the seas, the letter of the month is Zayin which suggests movement and a weapon of battle. The Torah, which we receive in this month, contains both the final spiritual goal of Creation and also the path of pursuit, the Mitzvos which cause us to grow. Sivan and Shavuos thus represent both the repose of Savua, and the dynamism of growth. This is the 'twin' (Gemini) idea of Sivan: the paradoxical coincidence of opposite qualities.

To truly live a 'twin' life and harmonize our own paradoxes, we (the unifying third element in the equation) need to subtly balance our insatiable desire for growth and perfection and the underlying satisfaction that we essentially already have and are. True wholeness integrates toil and yearning with unconditional joy and satisfaction.

COUNTING / STRIVING TO GET TO A SPACE
BEYOND ALL COUNTING

Connecting Pesach with Shavuos is the counting of the Omer. Inherent within the counting of these seven weeks are the two dimensions of striving and satisfaction, as above. According to many *Rishonim* / early commentators, one of the purposes of the act of counting was to teach a group of former slaves, who lived dictated by the rhythms of their masters, how to own and manage time. A deeper reason for the counting however, is to *count down* (See Ran, *Pesachim*, the end in the name of the Medrash. *Sefer haChinuch*, Mitzvah 273). Leaving Egypt, one knows that in 50 days one is going to receive the Torah. In great anticipation one counts down to that awesome moment.

Counting in this way gives voice to our striving and yearning, our seeking to get closer to our goal and fulfilment. As the days progress we get the sensation of becoming closer and closer to that moment of satisfaction. This is the place of movement and growth, and of 'eating' in order to fill a lack.

Yet, while the Torah tells us to count seven weeks, it also says we need to count 50 days: "And you shall count for yourselves... seven weeks... count 50 days" (*Vayikra*, 23:15-16). Why does the Torah say to count 50 days when in actuality we only count 49 days, which are seven weeks? (Tosefos asks this question. *Tosefos, Menachos*, 65b).

There is a paradigm in which we strive, yearn, work hard, and finally reach a point of rest. This rest is commensurate with the work that precedes it. It is like a vacation day; you work hard and then take a day off to rest, recoup and refresh. In this paradigm, rest and work are dependent upon each other; the quality of your rest is according to the strength of your work and the strength of your work depends on how well you rested.

Throughout the 49 days, the modes of work and rest, striving and attaining, are alternating; the seven 'rest' days of Shabbos are points of arrival and satisfaction within these seven weeks. When we finally reach a count of 49, we enjoy the completion of all our hard inner work. But then we go beyond all the cycles of causality and attainment to find ourselves in the 50th day.

This is a paradigm of paradox, one that is beyond causality, and which includes both work and rest simultaneously. 'Fifty' is the dimension of *Yovel* / Jubilee. In the Jubilee year slaves are freed and all properties revert back to their original owner. It is a time of true freedom and rest beyond the opposites of work and rest; it includes them both within a deeper context of deep rest.

Through the counting of individual units, we reach a place beyond counting, beyond yearning, as the Prophet says regarding Klal Yisrael, "And the *Mispar* / number of the People of Israel shall be as the sand of the sea, which cannot be… counted" (*Hoshea* 2:1). In other words, there is a *number* that indicates a reality *beyond* progressive numbers; a count that cannot be counted.

On the 50th day, Matan Torah, the holiday of Shavuos, we attain the level of 50; which is the numerical value of the word *Kol* / Everything (Chaf/20, Lamed/30 = 50). 'Everything' is a paradigm in which we sense the Keser, the overarching theme to our lives and how all of the individual details of our lives are contained within that context. From an 'Everything' perspective, all the details in our lives are contained and interconnected within a wholeness that is larger than the sum of its parts. This is the Keser of life, the Kol.

Torah is the Keser of the world. Perhaps for this reason the word *Torah* (in the singular form) appears in the Torah 50 times (*Rokeach, Devarim* 6:7). On the one hand, counting days is very much about each individual day, each distinct number, which is the idea of aspiring, working and yearning to get to the next day. On the other hand, the ultimate counting is to get to the end tally, the 50th day, the place of 'arrival' beyond yearning, working or striving, the freedom of the Jubilee.

This is the paradoxical nature of Sivan; 'movement' is simultaneous with restful 'satisfaction.' The word *Savua* and the number *Sheva* / seven represent *Aretz* / earth (from the word *Ratz* / running, moving) coexisting with *Shamayim* / Heaven (which can be read as *Sham Mayim* / there is water, 'there' implying stationary), body with soul, and spirituality with physicality, all in perfect harmony.

OWNING TIME

Counting numbers is progressive, one day leads to two days and then to three days. One cannot really count 'Today is the third day of the Omer' if he did not first count the previous two days. There cannot be a third without a first and a second.

Time, as numbers of units, is progressive and linear. There cannot be a present without a past, and there cannot be a future without the present. *Z'man* / time moves from the past into the future, moving, progressing. *Z'man* is related to the word *Hazmana* / to prepare or invite (*Sanhedrin*, 47b). Present time is moving from the past and preparing for a future.

Because it is progressive, time expresses yearning and desiring a future. We need to count time to move towards Shavuos. Yet, we are not merely counting time and then as a result reaching day 50, which is a paradigm beyond yearning and longing. By counting time we are 'creating' time and to create time we must already be above the rhythm and movement of time.

In order to create we need to be above what we are creating. Time, as explained, is progression and movement, and so, to create time would mean that we are standing above this rhythm and planted in a reality of stillness and non-movement, a place of 'satisfaction.'

If time is the paradigm of *Ratzo* / running, moving (*Ratz* / run being the root word of *Aretz* / earth, the below), to stand above time would mean to be in *Shamayim* / Heaven, the most stationary 'place.' In this way, creating time is the marriage of Heaven and earth, the Above with the below, the place of stillness together with the place of radical movement.

WHAT DOES IT MEAN TO 'CREATE TIME'

Regarding the holiday of Shavuos the Torah says, "You shall count for yourselves, from the day after Shabbos, seven weeks." Shabbos can either mean the seventh day of the week, the day traditionally called *Shabbos*, or it can refer to a day of Yom Tov, a holiday. For example, the Torah clearly calls Yom Kippur, "Shabbos of the Shabbos." The word *Shabbos* is also in the phrase, "You shall count for yourselves, from the day after *Shabbos*." This is a reference to the first day of Pesach. We count seven weeks from the day after the first day of Pesach, no matter what day of the week it is. If the first day of Pesach is Sunday, we count from Monday, and seven weeks and a day later will be Shavuos.

Centuries ago there was a faction of Jews called the Boeshusians, otherwise known as the *Tzedukim* / Sadducees, and later on in history called the *Keraim* / Karaites. During the Second Temple period (and once again, in early Medieval times) this faction of Jews adhered to the literal reading of the Torah and did not understand the *Mesorah* / living oral transmission of Torah via the Sages. When they read the verse, "You shall count for yourselves, from the day after Shabbos, seven weeks," they argued that it means literally the day after the Shabbos day of the seventh day of the week, and so, they counted the seven weeks always from the Sunday after the first day of Pesach. If the first day of Pesach was on a Monday, they would wait until the following Shabbos, and then begin to count seven weeks (*Menachos*, 65a).

There is a profound debate between the Sages and the Tzedukim, whether the Torah is exclusively a revelation from Above or has also been placed in human hands, below. The Tzedukim erroneously conjectured that Hashem revealed the Torah for us to follow simply and blindly. Our Sages received the insight that Hashem gave us the Torah for us to 'own': "At the beginning, the Torah is assigned to the Holy One, blessed be He, but at the end it is assigned to him [who studies it]" (*Avodah Zarah*, 19a. *Kidushin*, 32b).

One hint of this in Tanach is: כי אם בתורת ה' חפצו ובתורתו יהגה יומם ולילה / "In the Torah of Hashem is his desire, and in *his* (the person's) Torah he meditates day and night" (*Tehilim*, 1:2). When the Torah of Hashem is our deepest desire, it then becomes ours. We can assimilate within our minds Hashem's Torah in such a deep and integral way that we become like its owners.

This fundamental argument seeps into all areas of life, and in our context, it plays out in the question of the nature of time; do we, mortal and finite beings have any 'ownership' over time, or any right and ability to define it? Or is time exclusively 'owned' and defined by the Creator?

When the Torah asks us to "count seven weeks from the day after shabbos," which shabbos is this referring to? Is it the Shabbos of Hashem, the seventh day of the week, which Hashem designated and defined? Or is it the "Shabbos" of the first day of Pesach, the 15th day of the month? The beginning of the month was established by witnesses who came before the High Court of the Land of Israel and testified that they saw the new moon, in concert with the courts who could respond by establishing that day as Rosh Chodesh. This determined when the "Shabbos" of Pesach would fall. Today we do the same with our calendar system; in a certain sense we define and count time, as we were empowered to do. For the Tzedukim, "Shabbos" means Hashem's Shabbos alone; Hashem counts time and humanity can only follow.

The Seventh Day of Shabbos is an inherent truth of Hashem's world. The weekly cycle is not a contrivance of people, nor is it part of any astrological system or cycle in nature. There is no human need or reason to have seven-day weeks; they are created by Hashem. Weeks only exist because the Torah says they exist. Days and years too are dictated by the astrological structures designed by Hashem, they come automatically.

If you were lost in a desert and forgot what day it is, you would generally know by observing the sky; what phase of the day or night it is, whether it is spring or summer, and what part of the month it is. However, nothing will show you whether today is Tuesday or Wednesday.

The weekly cycle is Divine time. Hashem created the world in six days and rested on the seventh, establishing this set pattern for all time (*Ohr haChayim*, Bereishis). Shabbos, unlike Yom Tov, is not dependent on the calculations of man. Shabbos is Shabbos whether the high courts make a proclamation or not. Shabbos is called "holiness that comes on its own" — it is beyond man's participation.

For this reason, the Tzedukim who only believe in the Torah she-b'Kesav / Written Torah, Hashem's revelation, assert that we count from the seventh day of the weekly cycle; we must submit to Divine time.* A human being does not have the power to participate in 'creating' sacred time, for only Hashem creates time. All one can, and should, do is mark the passage of time as imposed upon us from Above.

---

* It is interesting to note that Karaites, who are closely related to the Tzedukim, continue to perform full prostrations in their daily prayers, in a mode of 'submission,' expressing an emphasis on human powerlessness.

Yet, our Sages received an oral tradition passed down through the generations from Moshe that Hashem gives us the power not merely to mark time, but to 'create time.' The Mitzvah to count the seven weeks is actually a Mitzvah to co-create the seven weeks, to co-create time. Through our counting, by the power of Hashem given to us in the Torah, human beings are determining the cycle of time; it is like a new structure, a new creation.

Rav Moshe ben Nachman (1194-1270), commonly known as the Ramban / Nachmanides, writes a puzzling statement. In Tractate Kiddushin our Sages speak about active Mitzvos that are time-bound, which women are exempt from performing, and active Mitzvos that are not time-bound, which women are indeed required to perform. 'Time-bound' means that they have a specific time when they must be performed, and not time-bound means Mitzvos that are always applicable. In listing some of the Mitzvos that are not time-bound, the Ramban (on *Kidushin*, 33b) writes that the counting of the Omer is *not* a time-bound Mitzvah. This is peculiar, as counting the Omer from Pesach until Shavuos is clearly a Mitzvah that has a very specific time zone (Shu't, *Avnei Nezer*, Orach Chayim, 384).

Perhaps the reason he writes this is that the Mitzvah to count seven weeks is not simply bound by time; the Mitzvah which is time itself (Shu't, *Seridei Aish*, 2, Siman 90) is to *create time* (see *Likutei Sichos*, 38, p. 14).

Hashem gives us the ability to create time, to form new structures and patterns in time. "From the day after shabbos," in this context, would not be speaking of the Creator's Shabbos, rather, from the shabbos that we, through our establishment of Rosh Chodesh, created. The power given to us at Mount Sinai includes counting from the day after Pesach, '*our* shabbos.'

By 'creating time' we demonstrate that we are essentially *above* time, above count. We are rooted in a place of *Savua* / satisfaction — timeless stillness and unity; and are thus able, through the power of the Torah, to create the 'movement' of *Shavua* / weeks. We are the 'owners' of time and time does not own us.

We are connected to *Hashem Echad* / the Oneness of Hashem, the unchanging calm and stability of *Shamayim*, Heaven. While rooted there, we can paradoxically lower ourselves into *Aretz* / the world of change, to sanctify it by innovating holy structures and patterns of time (*Tanya*, Igros Kodesh, 9).

Similarly with counting, we are able to count because we are above count and the paradigm of numbers: "And the number of the People of Israel... cannot be... counted" (*Hoshea* 2:1). We are counted; we are a *Mispar* / number, yet we are rooted in a place that cannot be counted.

Our ability to 'count' measure, and define reality, is our specialty. This is the reason why our Sages are called *Sofrim* / counters
"The / לפיכך נקראו ראשונים סופרים שהיו סופרים כל האותיות שבתורה
Rishonim / early Sages were called 'those who count' because they would count all the letters in the Torah" (*Kiddushin*, 30a). In essence they were *counters,* timeless structure-ers of time, space and consciousness, co-creators of the world.

Indeed, this is what the Oral aspect of the Torah, called *Torah she-b'al-Peh* / Torah of the mouth, is all about; creating sacred time and space through speech. (Although, in actuality, Mitzvos that are fully from our Sages do not create a *Cheftzah* / object of *Issur* / prohibition or Mitzvah, just an obligation on the *Gavra* / person. *Kesef Mishnah*, Hilchos Isurei Biah, 2:12. Teshuvas *Toras Chesed*, Orach Chayim, 31. *Asvan d'Oraysa*, Klal 10. *Minchas Eliezer*, 3:12. See also *Nesivas haMishpat*, 234:2)

What is unique about counting the Omer is that the obligation lies on all of *Klal Yisrael* / the Congregation of Israel, not just on the Sages or the High Court (*Menachos*, 65b). All of us need to participate in the creation of time, and through our individual countings, all of us together establish the holiday of Shavuos.

Counting is the special *Avodah* / spiritual-mental-emotional work of the previous month, the month of Iyyar, the month of the bull/of self-expression. (See the volume on the Month of Iyyar, where this is explained at great length.) The counting brings us a few days into Sivan, and then, at the end of the 49 days, there is a *Sach haCol* / the summation and culmination. The 50th day then, happens on its own. We do not count it, create it or even facilitate it — there is no human self-expression in it. Hashem, from Above, reveals the *Kedushah* / sanctity of the date that we confirmed would be Shavuos. Thus we receive the Torah from Above on this day.

Sivan is the month in which we received the Torah, the month of twins, the unification of the opposites of below and Above; counting and not-counting. While we count a few days this month, we also receive the *Sach haCol*, which is beyond counting and participation.

In Sivan, we enter the 50th level, corresponding to Binah, the consummate maturity of understanding. This 50th level of internal resting includes an 'intellectual resting' of our normal, mundane mind and way of thinking. It contains the intellectual openness and flexibility we need in order to receive the Torah, the Divine intellect. The illustrious Halachic decider, Rabbeinu Asher, known as the Rosh (1250-1327) writes (*Teshuvas haRosh*, Klal 55:9), that a person who becomes too familiar with natural or human-fashioned philosophies, will have a great difficulty comprehending Torah. In the words of the Rosh, כל הבא ונכנס מתחלה בחכמה זו לא יוכל לצאת ממנה להכנס בלבו חכמת התורה / "Whoever enters first the world of natural wisdom, cannot fully leave that world and allow the wisdom of the Torah to enter his heart." In our context, this would mean to receive the Torah properly, a person needs to rest their mind; to put their regular mind-set and manner of thinking to rest and open themselves up to the deep prophetic wisdom of the Torah.

After we work to achieve 49 levels of understanding, in order to receive the 50th level — which can only be granted as a gift from Above (*Rosh Hashanah*, 21b. *Nedarim*, 38a) — we must stop and rest in complete openness. For this reason, we count the 49 days between Pesach and Shavuos, and on the 50th day we cease counting and simply open ourselves in order to receive the gift of Torah.

OPENNESS TO 'RECEIVE' FROM THE 'MIND' OF HASHEM

This posture of total openness to receive the Divine influx of Torah is hinted at in this month's letter permutation of Hashem's Name (Yud-Vav-Hei-Hei), as discussed earlier. In the "natural" order of the letters (Yud-Hei-Vav-Hei), the Yud (seed of revelation) and Vav (channel of internalization) are separated and completed by the two Hei's.

The Hei's in the Divine Name function as vessels, way stations or circuit boards, which receive, process, digest, and transform the energy of the Yud before and after it descends down through the Vav. To get from the elevated point of Yud (the mind of Hashem, as it were) to the Vav (mind of man), revelation must pass through the processing station of the first Hei. Additionally, to get from the Vav, the mind of man, out into the world itself (creation) it must pass through the second Hei. The Yud (point) and the Vav (line) can be understood as representing the process of the actual light of revelation as it moves from Creator into creation; while the Hei's can be understood as the vessels through which revelation passes on its way to manifest expression. It is in the 'space' of the first Hei that the point of the Yud is processed and extended into the line of the Vav; it is in the 'space' of the second Hei that the line of the Vav is dimensionalized and expressed into actualization. The Divine Name can thus be understood as a lettristic depiction of the process of creation or revelation coming into being from 'the mind' of the Creator, through the mind of man, and out into the world through human speech or action.

Similar to the way in which kernels of wheat are processed into flour before we bake and ingest them, Divine revelation goes through a refining process before we receive it. We therefore do not receive the 'full hit' of raw revelation, as it is constantly being 'reduced' in order that we be able to digest it, so to speak. This is not the case in Sivan, and especially not on Shavuos. By moving the first Hei after the Vav, this gradual refining process is essentially collapsed, allowing us to receive the pure light of Hashem without any limitation or alteration. The pure light of the Yud comes straight down through the Vav with no intermediate process or period of digestion; we forego our normal 'processed grains' and go straight for the 'wheat berries' themselves. This occurs when we completely open ourselves to receive by *getting out of our own way*, by silencing our critical mind so as not to lessen, dampen or alter the light on its way into our soul on this night of revelation. That is why Shavuos is celebrated *not* (so much) as the night of "learning" Torah (49), but of "receiving" Torah (50). It is on this night alone that we are meant to receive the light of Torah unimpeded.

On every other day of the year we engage our critical consciousness in order to break down arguments and parse out meanings of details, this 'questioning faith' is in fact the prescribed way of Torah study. This is the world of 49, the path of active intellectual striving. On Shavuos however, the night of revelation, just as in a dream, we set aside our own conscious questions and critiques, allowing the light to just shine into us directly; inscribing itself onto the tablets of our heart, making its deepest impression within the subconscious depths of our soul. This is the level of 50, the experience of self-transcending receptivity. From there, it can then irrigate the sharp and distant corners of our mind throughout the rest of the year, bringing us to ever greater levels of comprehension and understanding. Paradoxically, this actively passive posture of pure spiritual reception is even harder for most of us to achieve than our normal process of active intellectualization. Shavuos teaches us that we must first deeply receive the Written Torah before we can responsibly and respectfully seek to understand its inner meanings through the conversational cauldron of the Oral Torah.

Although, of course, both the Written Torah and its oral dimensions are rooted and reflected within the *Ma'or* / Illuminator of the Torah (Yerushalmi, *Chagigah,* 1:7). This Ma'or is the actual 50th level of understanding, the 50th Gate. This cannot be humanly attained, only received. Although this *Source of Light* is beyond all grasp and comprehension, Its *Light* flows down from the 50th level of receiving into the world of 49, the world of intellectual pursuit. The 50th level thus includes both the revelation of the Written Torah and the concealed root of the Oral Torah.

The word *Torah* (in the singular form) appears in the text of the Torah 50 times. The Keser of Shavuos is the 50th level; we count 49 days, but the 50th day comes on its own (*Likutei Torah,* Shir haShirim, 35b). The number 50 symbolizes that which is beyond numbers or counting, it is the dimensionless dimension of Infinity, and thus total freedom. The freedom of slaves (as in the Jubilee year) is a metaphor for our freedom from the *Yetzer haRa* / negative inclination. It is also a metaphor regarding our ultimate freedom from death, which briefly awakened within us at Mount Sinai, with the giving of the Torah.

WHITE FIRE & BLACK FIRE:
THE TWO DIMENSIONS OF TORAH

At Mount Sinai, the deepest Divine intelligence of the universe was given to us as 'black fire upon white fire': "עורה של אש לבנה, וכתובה באש שחורה / "skin of white fire and written with black fire" (*Medrash Rabba,* Devarim, 3:12. *Medrash Rabba,* Shir haShirim, 5:11. על גבי אש לבנה באש שחורה. *Tanchuma,* Bereishis, 1. There is also the opposite version, where it seems that it is white fire upon black fire. Yerushalmi, *Shekalim* 6:1. *Korban ha'Eida*, ad loc. *Sotah*, 8:3. *Zohar* 2, 114a. *Yalkut Shimoni*, Yisro, 280). In this visual description, 'black fire' means the Torah that is revealed to us; the actual letters on the parchment. The 'white fire' is the empty space that surrounds and fills the open spaces of the letters. Just as a Kosher Torah must have every letter written out clearly. In order for a Torah scroll to be Kosher it must have a white empty space around each letter. Two letters that are touching lacks white space and renders the Torah scroll not Kosher.

When the black fire 'emerges from' the white fire, each letter must be separate from the others. However, in the world of the white fire, the entire Torah is a seamless whole, for all of the white space is connected and unified.

Defined and separated black fire is a reflection of the outer de-fined level of Torah wisdom. The open, unbounded, white fire is a reflection of the 'infinite' inner Torah wisdom. Similarly, our ob-servable world of duality, the *Alma d'Pirudah* / world of separation, emerges from the space of *Ein Sof* / the Infinite One.

In the manifest black-fire world of duality, the world was creat-ed by a 'separate' Creator; and the level of Torah that was revealed in this world begins with the letter Beis, (*Bereishis Bara* — in the beginning G-d created....) Beis is the second letter of the Aleph-Beis, alluding to two-ness. 'The Torah of Beis' is the level of Torah that is revealed in the world of *Beriah* / Creation, a spiritual and conceptual reality where there is 'separation' and clear distinction between Creator and creation.

Torah comes from the word *Hora'ah* / teaching or lesson. By looking into the Torah, learning it, and delving into its 'black fire,' we know exactly what actions we are called to do and called not to do in this world. Yet, the 'black fire' Torah is an expression of the 'white fire' Torah, which is the Torah on the level of Aleph/one/ unity. In fact, the first letter of revelation at Mount Sinai was not Beis but Aleph, as in, *Anochi Hashem* / "I am Hashem." At Mount Sinai all the people actually heard was the Aleph from the word *Anochi* (*Zerah Kodesh*, Shavuos, p.40).

Deep within the black fire of the Torah, is the white fire of Torah, the Torah of Aleph, the Torah of the inner world of *Atzilus* / unity or 'emanation' (*Atzilus* begins with Aleph). In the spiritual, conceptual world of Atzilus, Hashem does not create the world as a separate entity in a paradigm of duality, rather, Hashem here emanates the world as a transparent hologram, as it were, which is utterly unified with its Source.

The 'Torah of the white fire' is the dimension in which we can perceive every word in the Torah as another name of Hashem, as the Ramban writes (Ramban, *Hakdamah l'Torah*. Zohar 3, 73a). The Ramban explains how we can divide words differently than they appear; the Torah was originally written as a single, extremely long word, and thus where each word begins and ends can vary. For example, if we divide the letters differently, the first three words of the Torah, *Bereishis Bara Elokim*, can be read as *Bereish Yisbara Elokim*. The level of Torah in which every word is another name of Hashem is called the 'Torah of Atzilus' (*Shaloh*, Shavuos, Torah Ohr, 34). As the Zohar (2, *Yisro*, 87a) teaches, not only do the letters in the Torah comprise various names of Hashem, the entire Torah is one long name of Hashem (See also *Zohar* 2, 124a. *Zohar* 3, 71b).

Today, it is impossible to read the entire Torah as one word, not just because of the way the empty space surrounding the letters appears to form word-breaks, but because of the 'final letters' which create definite endings to many words. The Torah contains 22 regular letters, plus five 'final letters' which are formed differently and replace their regular counterpart at the end of a word: final Mem (ם replacing the regular מ), final Nun (ן replacing the regular נ), final Tzadik (ץ replacing the regular צ), final Pei (ף replacing the regular פ), and final Chaf (ך replacing the regular כ). These five modulated letters are known by their acronym, ך'ף'ץ'ן'ם / *MaN'Tz'PaCh*.

If, theoretically, there were no modulated final letters, even when words were separate from each other one could still read them as a single continuous word. Imagine reading the present sentence as a single word (*imaginereadingthepresentsentenceasasingleword*). It is peculiar, but possible. This cannot work in Hebrew when there are modulated final letters involved. For example, the words *Es ha-Shamayim* can be read as one word, *Eshashamayim*. However, the words *Es haShamayim v'es* cannot form a single word because *ha-Shamayim* ends with the final Mem, which is a forced break before *v'es*.

These five final letters were introduced into the Torah after the eating from The Tree of Knowledge, writes Rav Shelomo Molcho. (Born 1500 CE in Portugal to a family of Morranos and was named Diego Perez; later made *Teshuvah* and returned to a life of Torah, and became a great Tzadik and mystic, and was killed *Al-Kidush Hashem* 1532 CE, in Mantua, Italy.) As Chavah and Adam ate from the Tree of Knowledge of Good and Evil, they internalized the concept of duality, opposites, and separation with all their five senses. They 1) heard the voice of the

snake, 2) saw the fruit, 3) touched it, and 4) tasted it. While Chavah and Adam did not use the sense of smell specifically, the senses
of taste and smell are directly related and taste incorporates much
olfactory information. The sense of separation that colored all five
sense perceptions also created the five separative final letters, which
represent the five *Gevuros* / dimensions of constrictive energy. Yet,
in the higher level of reality called Atzilus, in which the Torah is
still revealed as one with the Tree of Life, the entire Torah is one
word (R. Shlomo Molcho, *Sefer haMefuar*, p. 38-41), one undivided, seemingly infinite, non-conceptual Name of Hashem.

From the verse (*Devarim*, 32:3), כי שם ה' אקרא הבו גדל לאלקינו /
"For the Name of Hashem is called, ascribe greatness to G-d,"
our Sages understand that we need to recite a blessing ("ascribe
greatness to Hashem") before we learn Torah ("before the Name of
Hashem is called") (*Berachos*, 21a. Yerushalmi, *Berachos*, 6, 52a). When we
read and learn Torah, which is the *Kevod Hashem* / Glory of Hashem, as the Avudaraham (14th Century Spain) writes, we must ascribe
this Glory to Hashem by reciting a blessing.

Rav Elazar Azikri (1533-1600) composed a commentary to the
Yerushalmi *Berachos*, where he writes that when the verse above
describes learning Torah as 'calling Hashem's Name' this is meant
quite literally, as the Torah is the Names of Hashem (*Zohar* 3, 73a)
and is one great Name of Hashem. Therefore, when we are learning
Torah we are actually chanting Hashem's Name.

Torah of Atzilus, the white fire, the great Name of Hashem, is
the Torah as it is still overtly identified as the Tree of Life. The first
set of *Luchos* / tablets that we received were a physical represen-

tation of this reality. The Luchos were *Charus* / engraved within the stones. *Charus* is related to the word *Cheirus* / freedom. When we receive the Torah we become truly 'free' (*Avos,* 6:2). That is, we become free from the effects of eating from the Tree of Knowledge (*Shabbos,* 156a), re-enter Tree of Life consciousness, and thus become free of all Tumah, impurity, and *Yetzer haRa* / negative inclination (*Zohar* 3, 97b). Moreover, not only do we become free of negativity, but we make *Teshuvah* / a return to our state at the beginning of human existence, prior to the introduction of death and separation, prior to eating from the Tree of Knowledge. In this state we too experience immortality, freedom from the 'angel of death' (*Medrash Rabbah,* Shemos, 41). "I said *Elokim Atem* / you are angelic creatures, and all of you are angels of the Most High" (*Tehilim,* 82:6). Says Rashi (ad loc), "When I gave you the Torah, I gave it to you on the condition that the Angel of Death should not rule over you." At Mount Sinai we received the Luchos and became free from the entire posture of duality and mortality and became, once again, fully absorbed by Gan Eden, the world of Unity.

At Mount Sinai we are like Adam and Chavah / Eve in the Garden of Eden, prior to eating from the Tree of Knowledge, and completely absorbed within the Tree of Life (At Sinai, the impurity resulting from eating from the Tree of Knowledge departed. *Shabbos,* 146a. See also, *Avodah Zara,* 5a). In that idyllic pristine state we were like small innocent children and did not eat meat. To procure meat from an animal requires killing it, and death did not yet exist. Eating meat demands cutting, and chewing with the teeth, which are acts connected to *Din* / judgment and separation. This is yet another reason (*Derashos Chasam Sofer,* Shavuos) why there is a custom to eat milk and dairy on Shavuos. Milk brings us back to our collective infancy, as we were born at the Exodus from Egypt and only 50 days later were enwrapped and embraced within the Tree of Life, at the foot of Mount Sinai.

This is also the reason why Shavuos, in contrast to the other major holidays of Pesach and Sukkos, is Biblically a single-day holiday. Teaches the *Zohar* (3, 96a), just as Klal Yisrael is *Goy Echad* / a singular nation (as will be explored in great detail in Essay 9 below), the Torah is *Echad* / One Torah, and it is One with the One and Only. Torah is the unified Tree of Life — unlike the Tree of Knowledge of opposites and separation. As Shavuos is the revealing of the Tree of Oneness, it is one day.

WHITE FIRE IS REST, BLACK FIRE IS MOVEMENT

The white fire Torah is experientially a state of *Menuchah* / rest, as the *Sefas Emes* (Shavuos) writes, total fulfilment and stillness, as there are no opposites and thus no yearning borne of separation. White fire is revealed unity; there is nowhere else to move or expand. It is spiritual perfection and immortality. The black fire aspect of Torah is a state of dynamic movement and growth. This is the way the Torah is revealed in this world of apparent duality, a world of distinctions, past and future, you and me, light and darkness, life and death, pure and impure.

Yet, clearly, the fullness of Torah includes both white parchment and black ink, the white fire and the black fire. The fullness of the Torah is the harmonization of Infinity (white fire) and finite distinctions (black fire). The Torah is One with Hashem. Just as Hashem is, *K'viyachol* / so-to-speak, neither finite nor exclusively infinite, but rather beyond and including both finitude and infinity, the same is true with regard to Hashem's Torah.

In the month of Sivan, the month of the Twins, the Torah was given. Being the month of both movement (the sense of walking and counting) and the month of satisfaction (resting, letting go of counting and striving) it is the opportune time for the revealing of the Torah.

The white fire is the place of perfect *Yichud* / unity, the 50th level, where there is total freedom from inner and outer work. Here there is no reason to do or think anything in particular, because you have arrived. Yearning, longing, toiling, counting, striving, and thus doing and getting closer and closer are all phenomena within the world of seven and 49, the Torah of black fire.

On every Shavuos night, just as in the historical moment of Matan Torah, there is a revelation of the entire Torah; both the white fire of Torah and the black fire of its expression. The black fire is all its narratives and Mitzvos and moral guidelines, its conceptual modes of description and communication. But none of these could be perceived without the contrast of the indescribable non-conceptual Infinite Light surrounding and illuminating them. Nor could the white fire be communicated without the contours of the black fire. The two are mutually dependent.

Collectively, we only heard the first two of the Ten Commandments at Mount Sinai (*Makkos*, 24a): "I am Hashem" and "You shall not have any others." These are the basis of the entire Torah, the roots which give life to all its details (*Tanya*, 20). The root of all positive Mitzvos is the awareness that "I am Hashem," and the root of refraining from all negative Mitzvos is the awareness that 'there is no other.'

An even deeper perspective on the revelation, in the name of Rebbe Mendel of Rimanov, is that collectively we only heard the first letter of the Ten Commandments: the Aleph of *Anochi* / "I Am" (*Zerah Kodesh*, Shavuos, p. 40). What we experienced at Mount Sinai is the absolute Oneness (Aleph) of Hashem, which is also the oneness of the white fire and black fire, the spirit and the law of the Torah. Both Divine silence and Divine speech are revealed in the Aleph of all-inclusive oneness. At that moment of revelation, wherever we looked, within every creature and thing, within all the 'black fire' of life and all the transcendent 'whiteness,' within every perception, we beheld only the Oneness of Hashem, the essence of *Anochi* / I alone Am.

THE 'WHITE FIRE' EXPERIENCED PRIOR TO MATAN TORAH

On Rosh Chodesh, the day Klal Yisrael reached Mount Sinai, says Rav Yosi, Hashem did not convey to them any preliminary directions, due to חולשא דאורחא / "weariness of the journey" (*Shabbos*, 86b).

Could it be possible that "weariness" rendered them incapable of hearing their Divine directives? Klal Yisrael had been yearning for this day of arrival, with anticipation and excitement, counting the days from when they left Egypt to when they would begin to receive Hashem's communications at Mount Sinai. And now, when they finally arrive at the foot of the Mountain, their 'introductory meeting' is cancelled just because they feel tired? In fact, we do not find any other point in their journey, neither when they were running out of Egypt in great haste, nor after the great ordeal at the Splitting of the Sea, that they needed to take a break and get rested. Even so, was Hashem really 'unable' to communicate with them and give them a Mitzvah or two while they were resting?

Furthermore, the next *Pasuk* / verse seems to contradict the premise that they needed rest: אתם ראיתם אשר עשיתי למצרים ואשא אתכם על־כנפי נשרים ואבא אתכם אלי / "You have seen what I did to the Egyptians, and [how] I carried you on eagles' wings, and I brought you to Me..." (*Shemos*, 19:4). Klal Yisrael was flown out of Egypt, so to speak, they were carried as if on the wings of eagles; so why would they be tired?

On a deeper level (see also *Likutei Sichos*, 28, p.7), the fact that Hashem did not speak to them or issue a command, means that there was no 'movement'; nothing being conveyed from the 'outside,' and no commandment to move forward or perform a certain action. However, in their stillness at the foot of Mount Sinai, something much more internal and meditative could have been achieved.

Perhaps the absence of a Divine utterance was not due to the 'weariness of the journey' literally, but rather because they were weary of the *concept* of journeying — they attained a level beyond the paradigm of journeying and moving. They were resting in the spiritual apex beyond progressive stages and steps. They had reached a place of Unity that is beyond 'here' versus 'there'; revealing the unmovable depths of their soul, their deepest truth, their oneness with the One.

Regarding that day the Torah tells us ויחן־שם ישראל נגד ההר / "And Israel encamped there opposite the mountain" (*Shemos*, 19:2). Grammatically, since the Torah is speaking of a collective group of people, all of Klal Yisrael, it seemingly should have said ויחנו / "encamped" in the plural, but it says ויחן — in the singular. Say our Sages, the singular form, denotes that they encamped there, "as one person with one heart" (*Mechilta*, Rashi ad loc).

On that day, the very first Rosh Chodesh Sivan to be celebrated in the history of Klal Yisrael, they reached a place of *Achdus* / unity within their own lives, with others and with the Creator of All Life.

There was nowhere further to travel, there was nothing to be said, and there was nothing to do. They arrived at No-thing-ness, Ayin, *Bitul* / the transparency of ego and sense of separate self; they did not even relate to 'journeying.' They did not need to be 'told' anything.

BEYOND *AYIN* AND STILLNESS

This state of Klal Yisrael at the foot of Mount Sinai, the *Bechinah* / condition of Ayin, is in a sense like white fire without any connection to black fire. It is a *Menuchah* / rest that is 'separate' from the world of doing and duality. This is a world 'beyond' creation, beyond expression, movement, defined meanings and words; beyond the world of black fire.

A few days later they reached an even higher level within Keser (beyond Ayin), in which there was a revealing of how all the black fire of reality is really one with the white fire. They realized that all *Yesh* / manifestation of existence is ultimately one with the Ayin, and rest is one with movement. They were shown that Hashem is the Creator of both Yesh and Ayin.

At Matan Torah there was a sweeping in of all of creation; everything was gathered in and enfolded within the white fire of the Torah, the *Anochi Hashem*. All phenomena sensed *Anochi Hashem*. This was a revelation of the white fire, and how all of the black fire is one with the white fire, as well as an expression of it.

At Mount Sinai, what was clearly revealed was the Ten Commandments. These ten are the roots of all the Mitzvos of the Torah, as Rav Sa'adia Gaon (10th Century) demonstrates how all the commandments can be categorized into ten groups, based on the Ten Commandments. We can understand this from different perspectives, each of them true:

A) If Klal Yisrael heard the first two of the ten: *Anochi Hashem* / "I Am Hashem..." and "Do not have any other gods..." then we can view these two as the source of all the commandments. In this perspective, the root of all positive commands is in *Anochi* and the root of all negative commands is, "Do not have any other gods."

B) If Klal Yisrael heard only the first command, indeed *Anochi Hashem* is the root of all Mitzvos (*Maor vaShemesh*, Yisro).

C) If all they heard was the Aleph, the *Oneness*, then we can view *this* as the root of all commandments.

D) If all they heard was the 'silence' before the sounds, then we can understand this pure white fire as the root of all the Mitzvos.

Each of these perspectives shows that there was a revealing of the Keser of creation, the inner purpose and objective of this manifest world and the Mitzvos that allow us to elevate ourselves along with the world, and demonstrates how all the black fire of creation is one with the white fire of creation.

THE TIKUN OF THE NIGHT OF SHAVUOS

The *Mekubalim* / Kabbalists of the 16th Century instituted a custom to recite a *Tikun Leil Shavuos*, a special collection of verses, on the night of Shavuos, to prepare for the receiving of the Torah. Essentially, one recites the first three and last three verses of all the portions in the 24 books of Torah, Prophets and Writings. Then one continues with the first and last Mishnayos in each of the tractates of the Mishnah — sweeping through the principle teachings of the oral tradition of the Torah. Then one concludes with a list of all the Mitzvos and a few passages from the Sod of Torah, the *Zohar* and *Sefer Yetzirah*. Through reciting the Tikun it is, "considered on High, as if one learned the entire Torah, both the entire written Torah and the entire *Torah she-b'al-Peh* / Oral Torah" (*Derech Pikudecha* [Dinov] Hakdamah 3, Os 4).

In the writings of Rav Yitzchak Luria (1534-1572), known as the Arizal (an acronym for "the G-dly Rabbi Yitzchak of Blessed Memory"), it is written, "In order to draw down the Keser... begin by reading (the Parshah of) Bereishis... and from there read the three beginning verses and three end verses of every *Parshah* / Torah portion… and then the *Nevi'im* / Prophets in the same manner… until the end of the Book of Chabakuk. Then the rest of the night (learn) the secrets of the Torah and the Zohar" (*Sha'ar haKavanos*, Shavuos). In other words, the main objective is the reading of the *TaNaCh*; the beginning and end verses of Torah, Nevi'im and *Kesuvim* / the Writings. When this is complete and there is still more time to the night, then one can continue learning the secrets of the Torah until *Alos haShachar* / the first light of dawn.

The Mitteler Rebbe teaches (*Sefer haMa'amarim*, Shavuos, p. 326), that a person should recite the *Kesav* / written Torah aspects of the Tikun prior to *Chatzos* / midnight, (then go to the Mikvah) and then, after Chatzos learn the Torah she-b'al-Peh / oral aspect of the Torah. The Zohar tells us that on the Night of Shavuos we should learn Torah she-b'al-Peh (*Zohar* 3, 97a. *Shulchan Aruch haRav*, Orach Chayim, 494:3).

In general, Torah she-b'al-Peh is connected with the night (*Zohar* 3, 23). The Medrash (*Yalkut*, Ki Tisa, at the end) reveals that Hashem taught Moshe Torah she-b'Kesav by day and by night Torah she-b'al-Peh, and this is how Moshe knew whether it was day or night. Throughout the year we are guided to not study or 'recite' Torah she-b'Kesav at night before *Chatzos* / halachic midnight (Mishnah Berurah, *Orach Chayim*, 238, Sha'arei Tziyon, 1), rather we are to study only Torah she-b'al-Peh during this time (Arizal, *Sha'ar haMitzvos*, VaEschanan. Zohar 98a). This is because she-b'Kesav has the quality of *Din* / judgment, and she-b'al-Peh has the quality of Chesed. For example, she-b'Kesav says that for certain crimes one receives 40 lashes, while the she-b'al-Peh clarifies that it means only 39 (Shu't *Avnei*

Tzedek, Yoreh De'ah, 102). As night is already an expression of Din, we do not want to strengthen it and create an imbalance. However, the custom of studying Torah she-b'Kesav on Shavuos night is a special case; there is a custom specifically to study she-b'Kesav until Chatzos. On this night there is an inclusion of black fire (Kesav) in the realm of white fire (b'al-Peh); there is a transcendence of left column energy (Din) and the right column energy (Chesed), and the inclusion of Din within Chesed.

PURPOSE OF THE TIKUN:

What is the purpose of the *Tikun Leil Shavuos*? On one level, as mentioned, the Tikun is a 'sampling' of the Tanach, Mishnah, Mitzvos, along with the Zohar and Sefer Yetzirah. However, the root of the Kabbalistic custom of Tikun Leil Shavuos is from the *Zohar*. To quote: "Sit my dear friends, sit, and let us innovate on this night a Tikun (an array of ornaments) for the Bride (the Sefirah of Malchus, which is associated with the *Shechinah* / Feminine Divine Presence and is also called *Knesses Yisrael* / the collective essential soul of Klal Yisrael). For anyone who participates with Her on this night (the night of Shavuos) will be protected Above and below for the entire (coming) year, and will pass through (live out) the year complete" (*Zohar*, Hakdamah, 9a).

This, then, is another purpose of the Tikun Leil Shavuos: to adorn the 'Bride' with 24 ornaments, which are the 24 books of Tanach. When Chavah (who is also associated with Malchus) was adorned by Hashem before her wedding* to Adam (*Zohar* 3, 79a), the

---

* The main spiritual work during the Sefira period is the Tikun of ZA / *Zeir*

Pasuk says ויבאה / *vaYevi'eha* / "He (G-d) brought her to Adam" (*Bereishis*, 2:22). Numerically, *vaYevi'eha* is 24. Later on, the Snake tried to cause a fall in Chavah and thus Hashem says, "ואיבה /*V'ei-vah* / I will place enmity between you and her" (*Bereishis*, 3:15). The phrase, "And I will place enmity" / ואיבה is also numerically 24 and contains the exact same letters. These are the 24 negative 'garments' mentioned in the prophets (*Yeshayahu*, 3:18-24). At Matan Torah we get rid of the negative influence of the Snake (*Shabbos*, 156a), and of the 24 negative garments or ornaments, and we are absorbed by the 24 books of the Tanach. All of this only explains the reason for reciting from the Tanach; why do we also recite from Mishnah and the other selections of the Oral Torah?

Another general reason that we recite a sampling of the entire Torah is to create a *Tikun* / repair, rectification, reintegration and assimilation of all the Torah that we have learned throughout the year, and open ourselves to receive Torah on an even higher level.

When the Divine intelligence first entered the world, it was an utterly simple seed; the entire Torah was encapsulated within the Aleph (or even just within the 'silence' that precedes the pronunciation of Aleph), the first letter of the first word revealed at Mount

---

Anpin, which are the *Midos* / personal and cosmic attributes, drawing down *Mochin* / higher consciousness from Binah and Chochmah during the counting, and finally from Keser on Shavuos. Yet there is also clearly an elevation of Malchus as well. The 24 books of Tanach correspond to the 24 ornaments of the Bride (Malchus), as the Arizal explains (*Sha'ar haKavanos*, 127c. *Sha'ar Ma'amarei Rashbi*, Naso, 54c). And as the Zohar (*Zohar* 3, Emor, 98a) teaches, on the night of Shavuos we create ornaments for the Bride, which is the Shechinah. This implies that the full Tikun of ZA is when it is elevated and there is unity between all the Sefiros, from the highest, Keser, to the lowest, Malchus.

Sinai. This is the *Klal* / principle or 'white fire' of the Torah — the Torah as one word, one letter, as one unified state, and as the revealed Name of Hashem.

This is the place of Torah where all the 'black fire' is still enfolded within a context of the 'white fire'; where all the details of Torah are absorbed within the Klal.

From this original Klal, this 'white fire' of Oneness, the Torah began to flower into 'many-ness,' into the world of 'black fire,' duality and apparent separation. The first letter Aleph became the first word *Anochi*, and then the first word became the first sentence, known as the first of the Ten Commandments, which expanded into the first two Commandments and then into the Ten Commandments. These ten sentences were then articulated as the 613 Mitzvos and as the thousands of words contained within the Five Books of the Torah, and the countless meanings, lessons, applications, complexities and Prat*im* / details of Torah wisdom that can be extrapolated from the Torah.

Following the conclusion of the Written Torah, Torah wisdom was given over to its most dedicated human adherents to innovate and be *Mechadesh* / creating newness within Torah. This is the Oral Tradition of the Torah.

THE KLAL & PRATIM OF THE TORAH

The power to co-create and reveal Torah comes from the Torah itself. Our Sages tell us: כל מה שתלמיד ותיק עתיד לחדש ניתן למשה בסיני / "Every *Chidush* / authentic innovation in Torah revealed by a dedicated student, was given to Moshe at Mount Sinai (*Yerushalmi*, Peah, 2:4. *Medrash Rabbah*, Koheles, 1:9, 2). This teaching seems paradoxical; if it is an innovation, how was it 'given'? And if the insight was really given on Mount Sinai originally, how is it a Chidush?

At Mount Sinai, the Torah was revealed as a Klal, but the Pratim were not yet fully revealed, although they too were all given at Mount Sinai (*Sotah*, 37a: "Just as Shemitah, its general principles and finer details, were all stated at Mount Sinai, likewise, all [Torah] was stated — general principles [together with] finer details—at Mount Sinai" (*Toras Kohanim*, 25:1. Rashi, first Pasuk in Behar). Even according to the opinion that the Pratim were given at Mount Sinai as well, they were revealed as being enfolded within the Klal). At Mount Sinai they experienced the white fire of the Torah; they heard *Anochi Hashem* and they sensed that everything, all Yesh, is nullified to the Ayin, and that both Yesh and Ayin are Hashem's creations.

When we employ our creative process of ingenuity and innovation, while staying true to the original Klal and Klalim / general principles of the Torah revealed at Mount Sinai, our innovation too can become an actual expression and articulation of the Divine revelation at Mount Sinai.

Our Sages tell us a fascinating story, "When Moshe ascended on high he found the Holy One, blessed be He, engaged in affixing crowns to the letters of the Torah. Said Moshe, 'Master of the Universe, who is restraining Your hand (from giving the Torah without these additions)?' Hashem answered, 'There will arise a man, at the end of many generations, Akiva ben Yoseph, who will expound from each dot (of text) heaps and heaps of laws.' 'Master of the

Universe,' said Moshe, 'permit me to see him.' He replied, 'Turn around.' Moshe (was projected in time centuries later and came to the school of Rebbe Akiva, and) went and sat down behind eight rows to listen to Rebbe Akiva. Not being able to follow the discussion, he was ill at ease. When they came to a certain subject, the disciples asked their teacher, 'Rebbe Akiva, From where do you know this idea?' Rebbe Akiva answered, 'It is a law given to Moshe at Mount Sinai,' and Moshe was comforted" (*Menachos*, 29b).

How is it possible that when Moshe heard Rebbe Akiva teaching and was not able to follow, he was "ill at ease"? Was Moshe, the most humble of men, jealous of Rebbe Akiva? When Rebbe Akiva reported, "It is a law given to Moshe at Mount Sinai," Moshe was then comforted. Why only when Rebbe Akiva mentioned that the roots of his ideas came from Moshe at Mount Sinai, was Moshe appeased? Does this story betray some kind of arrogance, G-d forbid?

What was really going on is as follows. Moshe received the great Klal and all the *Klalim* / principles of Torah at Mount Sinai, but the Pratim, including the Chidushim of our Sages throughout the ages, were not yet revealed at Mount Sinai. Therefore, Moshe asked Hashem to let him peek into a future generation in which a revered sage would expand upon the crowns of the letters of the Torah. He was projected into the future, to the academy of Rebbe Akiva, but he could not follow the arguments within Rebbe Akiva's teachings. What worried Moshe was not that he could not follow the stream of logic, but rather that the Pratim had perhaps veered so far from the Klal, and the creativity of the Sages had so digressed from the Klalim, that they had taken on a life of their own and were no longer rooted in the Klal of Torah which was revealed at Mount Sinai. This is why Moshe was ill at ease. When Rebbe Akiva answered his students that the foundation of the ideas comes from the Klalim revealed through Moshe at Mount Sinai, he was comforted.

Every generation has its own unique revelations of Torah that are specifically specialized to that generation; these are teachings which have not, and could not have, been revealed until their time. A perfect example of this: the Torah forbids a Moavite convert from marrying an ordinary Jew. The Yerushalmi teaches that in the times of Ruth there was a dispute among the sages regarding the parameters of this prohibition, and had she come earlier, she would not have been accepted (אילו באת אצלו מאתמול שלשום לא היינו מקבלין אותך *Yerushalmi*, Yevamos, 8:3). In fact, Boaz's uncle, Tov, subscribed to the stricter opinion, whereas Boaz belonged to a group of sages who utilized Torah she-b'al-Peh to determine that this prohibition only applied to male converts and not female converts like Ruth (*Medrash Rabbah*, Ruth, 7:7). The Gemara (*Kesubos*, 7b) says that Boaz assembled ten sages to publicly announce this Halachic decision, and only afterwards did he proceed to marry Ruth. It is due to this that we owe the birth of King David and all his lineage. Indeed, in every era there arises new understandings of Torah, which are revealed from Heaven, that are perfectly aligned with the needs of the generation (*Chidushei HaRim*, Hazinu, 266).

Moshe is instructed to fashion two silver trumpets to gather the Jewish people. Upon this, the Medrash (*Sifrei*, on Bamidbar, 10:23) teaches, "all the vessels which Moshe made were valid for him and future generations, save for the silver trumpets, which were only valid for him and not for future generations." This is because the trumpets were fashioned to gather and galvanize Klal Yisrael, every generation needs their own trumpets, unique to that generation.

Yet, deeply woven into the fabric of the many Pratim (the Chidushim that continue to be revealed) is the memory of a Klal, an all-inclusive source. Everything and everyone yearns to return to its Klal. We ourselves may long for the simplicity and innocence of our childhood, or for a primal state of wholeness, or to be included within the 'Klal' of a group identity. The deeper spiritual instinct behind this yearning is to embrace ourselves and others in non-dual awareness, in the unitive 'white fire.' Ultimately, we seek to bring all of creation back with us to the One; the means to this ultimate accomplishment is the Divine intelligence transmitted through the Torah.

Tikun, as in *repair,* means to ensure that the Torah is connected to the Klal of the revelation at Mount Sinai. On Shavuos night, prior to receiving the Torah once again, when we recite the Tikun Leil Shavuos, we are not literally 'studying' Torah, rather, we are sweeping through the texts and gathering together the Torah's Pratim into a unified state. We are collecting and returning the Pratim of Torah, which we have learned during the entire year, back to their source, the Klal. We are ensuring all the Torah which we assimilated with our own intellect, all the Chidushim that perhaps we created, are all securely rooted in the 'white fire' of Torah, the Aleph, and even the silence beyond the Aleph.

In general, the way we learn Torah is from Pratim to Klal; we begin in the details, with questions, uncertainties and debates, and through exertion and intellectual vigor we fit many small puzzle pieces together until we arrive at a resolution and a new Klal is revealed. Thus we move from darkness to light, from questions to answers, from Pratim to Klal.

This is the paradigm of אין אדם עומד על דברי תורה אלא אם כן נכשל בהן / "A person does not really understand the words of Torah (the Klal) unless he first stumbles in them (the Pratim)" (*Gitin*, 43a). This is the way our logical/sequential brain works. And this is the way of the world, ויהי־ערב ויהי־בקר / "There was night then there was day." This is the Torah apprehended via the brain and body. Yet, there is also a form of Torah-understanding connected to the Neshamah. This is the level of Torah that precedes birth, Torah that "enlightens" us when we are in the womb:

ונר דלוק לו על ראשו וצופה ומביט מסוף העולם ועד סופו ומלמדין אותו כל התורה כולה

"A candle is lit upon his head, and he can see from one end of the world to the other... and he is taught the entire Torah" (*Nidah*, 30b).

This can be called the Torah of Light. On this level there is first a revelation of the Klal, the *Kol haTorah Kulo* / entirety of all Torah. "A candle is lit upon his head" suggests the level of Keser, which is, "the crown upon the head." This light of clarity manifests immediately, without needing first to process details and climb through many levels of understanding. This is the Klal of Torah which we receive on Shavuos night, the Keser of Torah, the understanding of our Neshamah. Since to receive this there are no strenuous debates or maze of details, the 'left brain' quiets down as the night of Shavuos progresses, and we become more open and receptive for the revelation of the Keser of Torah.

On Shavuos Night we create a Tikun for all the Torah learning we engaged in throughout the year. Practically, we do this by swiftly reciting passages from various verses of Torah, Prophets and writings. These represent the *Torah she-b'Kesav* / written Torah, which is the Klal of the *Torah she-b'al-Peh* / Oral Torah. Thus when we proceed to recite Mishnah and the Pratim of all the 613 Mitzvos, we are gathering all the details we have learned in the past, all the 'black fire' that has formed in our minds, and returning them into the Klal, the white fire. On Shavuos, says the *Zohar* (*Tikunei Zohar*, Tikun 19, p. 38b), we are unifying the Torah she-b'Kesav with the Torah she-b'al-Peh.

In addition to reading the Tikun, the act of remaining awake all night immersed in sacred words of Torah, makes us less left-brain dependent or intellectually inflexible. Merely banishing sleep from our eyes and staying in this heightened state allows us to become receptive to and internalize something of the Klal, the 'white fire' of Torah (see R. Chayim Vital, *Sha'arei Kedushah*, 4:2). The practice of quickly chanting Divine words and not going into the various implications of the text, coupled with the physical and mental fatigue of staying up, is conducive to experiencing a sense of transcendence and connection to the 'white fire.' When morning arrives, we pray and then read from the Torah about the Revelation at Mount Sinai. This Torah reading is not experienced as describing an event of the past, rather an expression of an ever-unfolding process continuing in the present moment.

When we hear the Torah on the morning of Shavuos it is metaphysically the event of Matan Torah itself. Chazal tell us (*Yalkut Shimoni,* Yisro, 271), "Hashem told the people of Israel, 'My children, read this Torah portion each year and I will consider it as if you are standing at Mount Sinai, accepting the Torah.'" It is not only *as if* we are receiving the Torah, rather, we actually *do* receive the Torah anew.

Everything that happened in sacred history, also happens now. We receive the Torah anew every day, as Hashem is the *Nosein haTorah* / the Giver, or *Giving* in present tense, of Torah. More specifically, on Shavuos morning when we read the Torah we are actually receiving the revelation of Torah anew.

On Shavuos morning we re-live the experience of Mount Sinai. There is a cosmic downloading of all the Torah and all the wisdom that we will unpack throughout the entire coming year. Each year on Shavuos we become a receptacle to hold more of the Klal and assimilate more of the Divine Transcendent wisdom into our hearts and human minds.

REVELATION OF COSMIC & INDIVIDUAL KESER

Our collective Matan Torah is the revealing of the inner purpose of Creation, the Keser of reality, as explored earlier. On a personal level, our receiving of the Torah on Shavuos is when our crown, our Keser, our unique purpose, is revealed to us. When we get a glimpse of what our deepest purpose in this world is, when there is such an inner revelation, there is a sense of urgency and movement, progress and growth — and simultaneously there is a sense of *Savua* / inner satisfaction, peacefulness and ease. There is a balance between movement and repose, between aggressive extroversion (as during

Iyyar) and humble introversion (as during Nisan), between Chesed and Gevurah. Shavuos is the epitome of Gemini, the Twins, in which opposites are unified. Matan Torah is a revelation of the essential Oneness of Above and Below, human intellect and transcendence of intellect, the spiritual and the physical.

SHAVUOS:
THE REVELATION THAT INCLUDES ALL OF REALITY

The revelation on Shavuos is an all-pervasive experience, one that permeates and influences all of reality. When the Torah was given, "birds did not chirp nor did oxen low nor donkeys bray... there was total silence" (*Medrash Rabbah*, Shemos, 29:9). The whole of nature was absorbing the revelation of *Anochi Hashem* / "I am Hashem." Today, the way we re-experience this total penetrating experience is by including physical acts, such as eating, in the sacred celebration of Shavuos.

All opinions agree that Shavuos, the day we celebrate the giving and revealing of the Torah, is partly *laHashem* / for the Transcendent One, and partly *Lachem* / for you, the latter meaning it is participatory and celebrative 'on our terms' (*Pesachim*, 68b). In other words, we must spend part of Shavuos immersed in study and prayer, but we should also be open to receive the physical pleasures of holiday feastings; the body must also be incorporated in the festivities. Although we are celebrating a Yom Tov of transcendent wisdom, deep understanding and Divine intellect, we need to ensure that the joy of the day permeates all levels of our being. This is another expression of including and unifying the physical with the spiritual, Heaven with earth, which is the ultimate objective of the Torah.

During Shavuos, and during the month of Sivan in general, we ought to think about the Torah wisdom we have learned in the past, and consider if we have integrated these teachings. We should make sure that we have truly 'received' them into our day-to-day lives. As we bring Torah 'down' into the details of life, we also need to consider whether our studies are consciously connected to the Giver of the Torah, to Mount Sinai and to the transcendent white fire.

What has the Torah taught you?
How has the Torah clarified your life-purpose?

Beyond the deep enjoyment and life-enhancing wisdom of our Torah study, the Torah itself is our link to Hashem. Torah study is not merely an intellectual pursuit, but a conscious connection to the *Giver* of the Torah. The Giver of the Torah is present at every moment and is continually giving us the Torah anew. Every day we recite a morning blessing that declares, "Blessed are You... Who *gives* us Torah," in present tense. We do not say, "...Who *gave* us the Torah (at Mount Sinai, thousands of years ago)." Every day, and every moment, the Torah is being revealed, and every moment that we are aware of this we can make a conscious connection and bond with the Revealer of Torah.

Do you sense the presence of the 'Giver of Torah'
within your studies?

There are not just two 'parties' involved, us and the Torah. We need to contemplate the 'third' element in the equation, the Creator who unifies us with the Torah. "Three knots are knotted with each other, Hashem, the Torah and the People of Israel" (*Zohar* 3, 73a). Every day before we start learning, we need to take a moment, recite a blessing and think about our connection to the Giver of Torah (Ran, *Nedarim* 81a. Bach, *Orach Chayim*, 47. *Tanya*, 41). Throughout our learning, we should pause and think about our connection, our *Deveikus* / cleaving, to Hashem. (This is called Torah *Lishmah* / for the sake of connecting to Hashem (Rambam, Hilchos Teshuvah, 10:5. *Degel Machaneh Ephrayim*, Vayetze. *Maor vaShemesh*, Vayishlach). Although, simply, *Lishmah* means for the sake of doing the Mitzvah itself (Rashi, *Berachos*, 17a). The *Rosh*, however, writes that *Lishmah* means to fully grasp and understand (Rosh, *Nedarim*, 62a. *Nefesh haChayim*, Sha'ar 4:11. *Ruach Chayim*, Avos, 6:1). And it means learning with intellectual relish. Rabbeinu Yonah (Avos, 2:14. *Rav Avraham Min haHar*, 14th Century) writes the same (*Nedarim*, 48a). Perhaps these reasons are not mutually exclusive, and we can experience Deveikus within the intellectual relish (Hakdamah, *Eglei Tal*), as the Divine animating force within everything is present specifically within its *Ta'am* / taste or distinct *relish*.)

In the learning and understanding of Torah we are using our intellectual powers, our human capacity to think, and yet, we are also simultaneously connecting ourselves to the highest/deepest possible *Yichud* / unity (*Tanya*, 5), unity with Hashem and with the transcendental light of *Keser*.

This is what occurs every time we learn Torah and certainly an appropriate Kavanah during this month of the revealing of Torah.

☾

♈ SUMMARY OF SIVAN

*T*HE NAME OF THIS MONTH IN AKADIAN MEANS *APPOINTED*, as this month is the appointed time for the Giving of the Torah. Why is this month appointed?

In the month of Sivan we integrate the humbleness of Nisan and the assertiveness of Iyyar. This paradoxical quality, naturally arising within the **season** of late spring, also stimulates an energy of intellectual openness to receive, which relates to the **element** of the month: the open flowing wind. Walking, the **sense** of the month, is also a movement which is both dynamic and restful. Such 'walking' requires the qualities of the left leg, the **body part** of the month, which allows us to move forward assertively while also being settled and satisfied with what we have. The **Parshios** of this month describe the journeys of Klal Yisrael in the desert, movement within stillness. This desert stillness is the setting for the earthly reception of the Divine teaching.

Also expressing the paradoxical integration of two polarities is the **sign** of the month, Gemini or twins, and the **verse** of the month alludes to two opposites that are united. The **tribe** of the month embodies the paradoxical joining of worldliness and spirituality. The **letter sequence of Hashem's Name** for this month is a diagram of the masculine and feminine facing each other like marriage partners who are different but unified for a greater purpose.

All the above describes the unique **holiday** of Shavuos, the Giving of the Torah, which merged Heaven and earth, spirituality and physicality, intellect and action, somethingness and no-thingness, Malchus / immanence and Keser / transcendence. This merging reveals the third element in uniting all opposites: *Anochi* / the all-inclusive Divine Essence. Inwardly, we can experience all of this in the practice of Shavuos night, staying up through dawn, performing the *Tikun Leil Shavuos.*

12 DIMENSIONS OF SIVAN

Sequence of Hashem's Name	*Yud-Vav-Hei-Hei* (Masculine and Feminine letters facing each other like marriage partners)
Torah Verse	*Y'dosav. U-l'tzela Ha-mishkan Ha-sheinis* (alluding to two opposites that are united)
Letter	Zayin, ז (numerically seven, alluding to weeks)
Month Name	Sivan (related to Akkadian word *Simanu* / appointed)
Sense	'Walking' (movement that is paradoxically restful)
Zodiac	*T'umim* / twins or Gemini
Tribe	Zevulun (joining worldly business and spirituality)
Body Part	Left leg (movement)
Element	Wind (freedom/intellectual openness)
Parshios/Torah Portions	Bamidbar, Naso, Beha'alosecha, and Shelach (journeying in the stillness of the desert)
Season	End of Spring (gratitude)

ׇׁ֗ק

PRACTICE:
The Art of Receiving

ESIDES THE *RECEIVING OF THE TORAH,* SHAVUOS IS ALSO
the Day of *Bikurim* / first fruits of the harvest. The
Mitzvah of Bikurim consisted of selecting the year's
first fruits, placing them in a beautiful basket, bringing them to the
Beis haMikdash / Temple in Jerusalem, and offering them to the
Kohen. (Prior to the Beis haMikdash the Bikurim were brought during the period of the Mishkan in Shilo. *Sifrei,* Ki Savo, 2.) This Mitzvah obviously did
not come into effect until Klal Yisrael entered the Land of Israel,
and only after it was fully conquered and settled (*Kidushin,* 37b).

Every Mitzvah is performed in, and functions within, the dimensions of time, space and consciousness. The main act of the
Mitzvah of Bikurim is the person taking his first grown fruits and

bringing them to the Beis haMikdash. Without a Beis haMikdash we cannot perform this action. Yet, within the dimension of consciousness, the inner aspect of this Mitzvah is always possible for us to perform.

When the month of Sivan comes along, we have already traversed the month of Iyyar, which is full of spiritual work, counting down to Shavuos and refining oneself and one's traits. When we finally arrive at this month, we are ready to harvest and 'receive' the fruits of our intense spiritual, mental, and emotional labors. After conquering and settling our entire 'Land,' ensuring that all our internal Midos and interpersonal attributes are 'settled' with *Yishuv haDa'as* / a settled mind, we offer our finest new 'fruits' to Hashem. Our newly refined emotions are thus directed upward, toward living a higher purpose, and we can truly begin to 'harvest' or 'receive' all our emotions in a holy and positive way. Also, in response to this 'offering' we receive new wisdom on Shavuos and because of this, our entire being and all our attributes are further transformed and sanctified.

On Shavuos morning we re-live the experience of Mount Sinai. For each individual there is a download of all the Torah-understanding and all the *Chidushim* / novelties of Torah that he will reveal during the entire coming year. We not only receive 'Torah wisdom' specifically, but we also receive all the *Seichel* / intelligence and inner knowledge that we will need in order to serve Hashem on a deeper level during the coming year. In this way, Shavuos is the headquarters of all our intelligence and learning, and over the course of the year we need to work in order to draw it down further and unpack what we have received.

On this morning there is a cosmic downloading of all the Torah and wisdom that all of Klal Yisrael will receive for the entire coming year — from the most accomplished living *Gedolim* / Torah geniuses, to the most innocent school children learning the Aleph-Beis, and from the person sitting next to you in Shul, to the lone Jewish outreach worker in a far-off land. On this day we rejoice not only in the wisdom and light that we ourselves will attain, but that of each and every person in the vast community of Yisrael. Knowing this fact multiplies our joy.

Shavuos, and the entire month of Sivan, is a time to hone the art of receiving, on all levels of our being. To receive, to become a vessel intellectually, spiritually or interpersonally, is an art that needs to be carefully learned and mastered.

Many of us are able to 'give,' and many of us know how to 'take,' but few have mastered the art of mature receiving. It is easy to give; it can even be selfish and ego-aggrandizing to do so. It's also easy to take. But to *receive* is an art. Receptivity is a way of making a *Yichud* / unification with the giver. Ultimately, being receptive is the greatest gift we can give to another; receiving empowers the giver.

RECEIVING WISDOM

To be open to receive new wisdom, we first need to empty ourselves, to make ourselves like a *Midbar* / desert. Why was the Torah given in a desert? Say our Sages (*Medrash Rabbah*, Shemos 1:7), to receive Torah we need to make *ourselves* into a desert, empty of all preconceived ideas and frames of reference. Only when we make ourselves like *Hefker* / ownerless, do we acquire the wisdom of the Torah.

We need to traverse the desert to get to Mount Sinai, and Mount Sinai itself is in that desert. The desert is a place of emptiness: "a land where no one travels and no one lives" (*Yirmiyahu*, 2:6). It is a place separate from the everyday reality. In order to open ourselves to receive and absorb a higher wisdom we need to be in this place of emptiness.

To enter this desert and attain a more profound level of understanding, we need to learn to surrender our conventional or previous ways of thinking. This is true with the attainment of all knowledge; how much more so with higher, Divine wisdom. To truly receive Torah we need to empty ourselves of what we *think* we know, drop assumptions about our world and our identity, and 'camp' for some time in this vulnerable, unfamiliar place of emptiness. Only when we can remain open to this 'void,' can we truly be filled.

We need to learn to say 'I don't know,' if we really want to know something that is beyond our grasp.

The Baal Shem Tov chose Reb Yechiel, known as 'the Deutschel' (the German), as the husband for his beloved daughter, Udel. Reb Yechiel had become known to the Baal Shem Tov as a great scholar, so he sent one of his own disciples to go and see if he would be a worthy addition to their inner circle. When the disciple found Reb Yechiel, he began testing him to observe his level of scholarship. All that Reb Yechiel said was, "I have not known, I do not know, and I will not know!" When the Baal Shem Tov received Reb Yechiel's answer, he was very happy and confirmed that Reb

Yechiel indeed belongs in Mezhibuzh with the inner circle of the Baal Shem Tov's students.

May our minds and hearts be completely open like Reb Yechiel, and may we merit to be proper vessels to receive the Torah, with joy and openness.

ת

PART TWO:
Essays on Shavuos & Matan Torah

ॐ
Essay One
—
FIFTY DAYS FROM SHABBOS OR FROM PESACH:
Receiving or Participating with Time & Torah

I F WE LOOK CLOSELY, WE SEE THAT THE TORAH IS STRANGELY ambiguous about the date and even the month of the Yom Tov of Shavuos. All the information we have in the *Chumash* / Five Books of Moshe is: "And you shall count for yourselves from after the day of *Shabbos* / rest, from the day that you brought the sheaf of the waving; seven weeks shall there be complete… count 50 days; and you shall present a new meal-offering unto Hashem… You shall bring out of your dwellings two wave-loaves… they shall be baked with leaven, for *Bikurim* / first-fruits unto Hashem" (*Vayikra*, 23:15-17).

This is not clear. We are only told to count seven weeks "from after the day of *Shabbos* / rest" and then there will be a couple special offerings. It does not mention a holiday connected to the giving of the Torah at all, it only mentions a day of *Bikurim* / first fruits. Yet, we know from another verse that the entire project of the Exodus from Egypt was for Klal Yisrael to reach the mountain and receive the Torah, as Hashem tells Moshe: "When you bring the nation out of Egypt, you will serve Hashem upon this mountain" (*Shemos*, 3:12). But why doesn't the Torah associate the day of Bikurim with the Giving of the Torah? Why doesn't it describe Shavuos clearly as a Yom Tov, as it does for the Exodus on Pesach, for example?

Regarding Pesach or Sukkos, in addition to their own agricultural identity, they are also spoken about in terms of commemorating the Exodus and the subsequent sojourn in the Desert. The Torah thus combines an agricultural season with a historical event, thus providing a deeply meaningful experience to the lives of the farmers. The Mitzvos related to that historical event are thus joined to palpable seasonal changes, which heighten our awareness and involve all our sensations and emotions. Shavuos, however, is unique in that the Torah does not clearly join the day with any historically monumental event. We do know, from the second verse above, that at some date after the Exodus there would be a certain Divine service on a specific mountain. Therefore the day of Bikurim is loosely associated with the time of the giving of the Torah — perhaps not to the date, but at least in close proximity.

All of this seems unsatisfactory; it is vital that we know exactly when Matan Torah happened, since as with all other holidays, the supernatural quality of the original event will be accessible on the same calendar date. In order to celebrate and reenact the Receiving of the Torah, we must know exactly when it happened.

Furthermore, the Torah says we need to count seven weeks from "the day after Shabbos." But what Shabbos is this referring to? It must be a Shabbos connected to Pesach, as the Pesukim before this Pasuk speak about the holiday of Pesach, but we are still left with a startling ambiguity.

Chazal and the oral tradition of the Torah tells us that in this context, "Shabbos" is not the seventh day of the week, rather it refers to Pesach itself. *Shabbos* simply means a day of rest, and sometimes the Torah calls a Yom Tov, "Shabbos"; such as Yom Kippur, which is called *Shabbos Shabbaton* / Shabbos of the Shabbos.

In another context, speaking about the law of reciting *Havdalah* / a blessing at the end of Shabbos or Yom Tov, the Rambam writes (*Hilchos Shabbos,* 29:18), "Just as we recite kiddush on Friday night and havdalah on Saturday night, so too, we recite kiddush on the night of a holiday's commencement and havdalah on the night following a holiday and on the night following Yom Kippur, שכולם שבתות ה' הן / for they are all Shabboses to Hashem." In other words, every Yom Tov is a form of Shabbos. "Yomim Tovim are also called Shabbos" / וימים טובים נמי שבתות איקרו (*Rashi*, Shavuos, 15b. די"ט נמי איקרי שבת. *Magen Avraham*, Orach Chayim, 488).

However, this brings us to the well-known argument between the *Tzedukim* / Sadducees (a group of Jews who lived during the second Beis haMikdash period who subscribed only to the literal written words of the Torah) and the *Pirushim* / Pharisees, which are Chazal. The argument is regarding the phrase, "from the day after Shabbos." Does this refer to the first day of Pesach, as according to the tradition and practice of the Pirushim? Or does it mean *Shabbos* literally, meaning that we should count after the first Seventh

Day within the festival of Pesach? The Tzedukim held this way and thus always celebrated the holiday of Shavuos on a Sunday.

First, the Gemara on this debate (*Menachos*, 65a-65b): "...Fasting is prohibited... from the eighth [of Nisan] until the close of the Festival [of Passover], during which time the date for the Feast of Weeks was re-established..." As above, the Boethusians (*Tzedukim* / Sadducees) held that the Feast of Weeks must always be on Sunday, the day after the Shabbos. But Rav Yochanan Ben Zakkai entered into the discussion, "Fools that you are! From where do you derive it?" Not one of them was able to answer him, save one old man who started babbling, "Moshe our teacher was a great lover of Israel, and knowing full well that the Feast of Weeks lasted only one day he therefore fixed it on the day after the Sabbath so that Israel might enjoy themselves for two successive days."

Countered Rav Yochanan, "If Moshe was a great lover of Israel, why then did he detain them in the wilderness for 40 years?" "Master," said the other, "like that you would dismiss me?" "Fool," he answered, "should not our perfect Torah be as convincing as your idle talk! Now one verse says, 'You shall number 50 days,' while the other verse says, 'Seven weeks shall there be complete.' How are these to be reconciled?" (The former verse speaks of counting 50 days irrespective of the completeness of *weeks*, while the latter verse speaks specifically of seven complete weeks.)

"The latter verse refers to the time when the [first day of the] Festival [of Pesach] falls on Shabbos (thus seven full weeks), while the former to the time when the [first day of the] Festival falls on a weekday (and therefore only on the 50th day)." This is what the Gemara records.

What is the deeper argument between these two groups? What does it mean "Moshe was a lover of Israel?" And what is the meaning of Rav Yochanan's answer — that if Moshe was a lover of Israel, why would he keep them in the Desert for 40 years? Does it imply that Moshe was not a lover of Israel, Chas veShalom?

This argument brings to the surface an even deeper question, 'What is the essential objective of the Torah?' The Sadducees had only accepted upon themselves the Written Torah, and were generally wealthy landowners; while the Perushim, who eventually became *Chazal* / our Sages, generally did not own land or agriculture and were not wealthy. The Perushim inherited the oral tradition of the Torah; many did have a trade, such as shoemaker or woodcarier, but they were mainly scholars.

As their daily lives were more based on agriculture, the Sadducees believed that the point of the Yom Tov of Shavuos was an agricultural celebration. It was a day to rest from working the land. Therefore, since Moshe certainly loved his people, he made sure that this holiday would fall out on Sunday, so that the people could have two days in a row off from work; Shavuos was essentially a long-weekend.

The Perushim, however, had the authentic *Mesorah* / tradition, which held that the purpose of the *Sefira* / counting of the seven weeks is to 'count down' to Matan Torah. Shavuos is not merely a long weekend of physical rest, but the day the Torah was given. Shavuos is the culmination of Pesach — much like Shemini Atzeres is the culmination of Sukkos, and thus Chazal gave Shavuos the alternate name *Atzeres*. The time between Pesach and Shavuos is therefore like an extended period of *Chol haMoed* / intermediate days of a long festival, as the Ramban writes (Ramban, *Vayikra*, 23:16). The Torah defines the culmination of Pesach, "When you bring the nation out of Egypt, you will serve Hashem upon this mountain." In other words, Pesach is completed with the giving of the Torah.

Thus Shavuos, countered the Perushim, is primarily a spiritual day rooted in a dimension beyond time and space, and it can fall on any day of the week. It is also a reality that is revealed within time and space, and so is it also celebrated with festive meals and physical rest.

This still leaves questions to be answered, mainly, why indeed is Shavuos, as the Yom Tov celebrating the giving of the Torah, not mentioned clearly in the Torah? The answer to this will reveal an even deeper meaning to the argument between the Tzedukim and Chazal.

CYCLICAL OR LINEAR TIME

Most ancients believed in cyclical time: what was, will be. They observed the cyclical patterns proliferating throughout creation — sprouting, blossoming, bearing fruit, wilting, lying dormant, and returning again to life — and concluded that time operates in an infinitely-recurring rhythm. The ancient thinkers referred to this phenomenon as 'the Eternal Return'; what occurred in the past will inevitably occur again, and again, for all eternity.

The Torah, and later more revealed by the Prophets and finally by Chazal, introduced a revolutionary way of observing and counting time. Sharp departing from the world-view of ancient cultures, the Torah revealed a linear and progressive dimension. In this view, time began at Creation, and we are steadily progressing in a continuous quest toward a Complete Redemption. This is a great gift; time progresses, and thus there is room for hope, change and a better future.

The Tzedukim were farmers, centered on seasonal cycles. What were the Torah's holidays to them, therefore, but celebrations of the seasonal cycles of the year. The Perushim were scholars, and looking into the deeper aspects of Torah they recognized the deeper progression of time. When they looked at the Yom Tov of Shavuos they understood that it was a culmination of Pesach, a progression from Pesach to the Giving of the Torah. The entire reason for *Sefiras haOmer* / counting the Omer is a countdown to Matan Torah, a spiritual day. (See volume on the Month of Iyyar for lengthy discussions on *Sefiras haOmer.*)

As we mentioned, the Tzedukim argued that Moshe was a lover of Israel, and thus gave us a two day weekend. What is the meaning of Chazal's response that, 'if Moshe is such a lover of the Jews, why did he keep them in the desert for 40 years?'

SHAVUOS: GIFTED OR WORKED FOR?

Not only did the Perushim recognize the 'progress' in time, but also that human participation was part of this progress. This issue comes into focus when we look closely at the issue of 'becoming free.'

There are two stages in becoming free: a) attaining freedom *from*, as in freedom from Egyptian slavery and oppression, and b) attaining freedom *to*, the freedom to choose; the freedom to live a higher, more responsible life, as revealed at Mount Sinai.

'Freedom' does not mean receiving something *for free*. In Egypt, as slaves, we ate for free, "We remember the grain we ate for free" (*Bamidbar*, 11:5). "Free" in this context means there is no relationship between one's work and the result, the food. There is no clear connection between the hard labor of a slave and what a slave is being fed. Thus, the food that is given is 'for free' or without participation.

Real freedom is to freely choose to live responsibly and authentically. It is not only to be free from oppression, persecution, or slavery; even under better conditions, a person can continue to inwardly be a slave. True freedom is the freedom of Matan Torah. At Mount Sinai we received the *Luchos* / Tablets which were *Charus* / engraved in the stone. *Charus* can be read as *Cheirus* / freedom (*Avos*, 6:2). We were free to live deeply responsible lives.

Pesach is bodily freedom, freedom of action and freedom from slavery. However, we are not entirely free until we reach the higher consciousness and deeper understanding manifested at Matan Torah. We become free when, through our insight, we accept the *Ol Malchus Shamayim* / the 'yoke' or service of Heaven. This Divine servitude is paradoxically 'freedom,' and we do not 'eat for free.' It requires hard work, but is more free than slavery, *because it is participatory*.

When, after Pesach, we finally complete our counting and inner work to reach Shavuos, there is a release of consciousness from all constriction. This is not merely a release from work, it is a positive freedom, an entering into the zone of conscious destiny and purpose.

In the first stages of a relationship, two people feel separate; they tend to tread carefully, anxious to please and not upset the other. When the relationship matures and they become like one, they are "engraved," instead of being like 'ink on paper.' They no longer feel anxious or alien. The more we accept the Ol Malchus Shamayim, the more we allow Torah to become one with us, the more free, and inwardly carefree, our life becomes.

B'chukosai Teileichu / "Walk in My *Chukim* / statutes," says the Pasuk, in the portion of the Torah read before the giving of the Torah on Shavuos. *Chukim* can also mean *engraved*. When something is engraved or 'ingrained' into your being, when the Torah has become one with you and you walk through life with it, you can have greater *Hispashtus* / expansion. As the Mei haShiloach explains the above verse (Bechukosai beginning), "Hashem is with you wherever you go," when you become one with the Torah.

And even if the journey to the Promised Land becomes a 40 year journey, when we understand the Torah and become one with it, 40 becomes a symbol of process, a fruitful period of work and eventual transformation.

This is the intention of Torah, and the true love of Moshe; to allow the other to 'work' on achieving their greatness. It is not to give 'for free' — that is ultimately 'slavery,' as the slave becomes dependent on the giver. If greatness is not earned it is ultimately disempowering; as with lottery winners, who tend to become bankrupt and depressed.

This is how the Perushim respond, "If Moshe was a 'lover of Israel' (perhaps) he would have not kept us in the desert for 40 years."

Meaning, Moshe did not want to give out a 'free ride,' a life of 'for free' as we had lived in Egypt. If he had, we would have gone right away into Israel even before we were fully ready. A true leader such as Moshe wants us to gain freedom on our own, to work for it. This is why we remained in the desert for 40 years, 40 being a period of self-transformation.

Of course Moshe is a lover of Israel, but love does not imply, for example, a parent giving a child a large sum of money if they demand it. Love would allow the child to build up a sense of worthiness and responsibility to receive the gift given. Then they can feel that it is not 'for free,' rather, they worked for it. This is not the same as suggesting to the child that they have to earn parental affection; to the contrary, this allows the child to realize their own worth from within, and gradually become self-empowered and free from dependency on others.

The 40 years in the desert means when they finally entered *Eretz Yisrael* / the Land of Israel, they truly desired it; they had created vessels for the experience. Once we had worked on our freedom, it was "engraved" in us and we could sustain it even when Moshe was no longer physically with us. This was real self-elevation; it was not simply the result of Moshe lifting us to a higher level. This idea is also connected to Shavuos. Even though Shavuos, as Keser, is humanly unattainable, we still need to work to elevate ourselves toward Shavuos. We need to count and *create* Shavuos.

Every year brings a new level of Matan Torah, and thus every year we need to count, yearn and work on ourselves again. Matan Torah does not come on its own; it is not always 'on a Sunday.'

We have to bring ourselves to the gate of the 50th day.

For the Tzedukim, Shavuos was a 'free gift' from Above, and nothing to do with human participation or labor. But Chazal refuted this: that is not real love. To love is to make the recipient a participant, to own the gift, and thus love allowed Klal Yisrael to wander and even make dramatic mistakes in the desert for 40 years; creating in them a capacity to enter Eretz Yisrael. Hashem's love for us allows us to participate in our 'entering' into the world of Shavuos.

A DEEPER LOOK: THE CREATOR'S TIME VS. OUR TIME

Also related to this fundamental debate is the fact that according to the Tzedukim, Shavuos would specifically always be on Sunday — and never, for example, on a Monday.

Shabbos on the seventh day of the week has a *Kedushah* / holiness that comes into the world on its own. It is מקדשא וקיימא / *Mikadshah v'Kaymah* / sanctified and established from Above, (*Beitzah*, 17a), in stark contrast to the weekdays, which is a time of toil and working the land. If we count the Sefira always from the seventh day, that is Shabbos, and Shavuos is always on the same day, then Shavuos would be a holiday in the same category as Shabbos, with the same characteristics.

There is a difference between the 'Creator's time,' which is the paradigm of Shabbos, and 'our time,' which is the weekday paradigm.

A basic divide between the worldview of the Tzedukim and Chazal is that the Tzedukim only believed in *Torah she-b'Kesav /* the written aspect of the Torah, the Divine revelation from Above; while Chazal also believed in the Oral Tradition, also revealed from Above, but through human beings. With their orientation, the Tzedukim naturally opted to count from the Shabbos that is given from Above. They felt that the *Koach /* power to count can only come from Shabbos, from the 'Creator's time.'

Chazal and the Pirushim held that Hashem gave us the Torah; the Creator fully transmitted the Torah to man. As mentioned earlier; "In the Torah of Hashem he desires, and in his Torah he meditates day and night" (*Tehilim,* 1:2). Our Sages comment, "At the beginning, the Torah is assigned to the Holy One, blessed be He, but at the end it is assigned to him [who studies it]" (*Avodah Zara,* 19a).

ORAL TORAH

HaKadosh Baruch Hu gave us the Torah to expand and reveal more and more insight,* all the while, keeping it rooted in the revelation at Mount Sinai. By using our minds in this way, we are participating in the giving of the Torah. The same is true with time.

---

* There is a Mitzvah to be Mechadesh / innovating new understandings of Torah (Alter Rebbe, Hilchos Talmud Torah, 1:1 "לחדש הלכות רבות" See, Zohar 1, 12b. Taz. Orach Chayim, 543:13. Tanya, Igros Kodesh, 26. Kesav Sofar, Hakdamah). The Mitzvah to "be fruitful and multiply" also applies to Torah. In the words of Rav Meir Papurish, וצריך ...בשכלו עקר יהיה שלא תורה בדברי ורביה פריה מצות שיחדש מה שלא חידש מקדמת דינא (Ohr Tzadikim, Hilchos Talmud Torah, Siman, 22:42). Indeed, קוב"ה חדי בפלפולא דאורייתא Although it does not have a clear source in Gemara or Medarash, it is brought down in the many Teshuvos of Achronim. For example, Shu't Shoel U'Meishiv, Mahadura Kama, Siman 167. Shu't Chasam Sofar 2, Yorah De'ah, Teshuvah 280; 7; 12. See also, Hakdamah, Ketzos HaChoshen. This statement is based on Zohar 2, 235a. 3, 59b.

Hashem gave time to us: *haChodesh haZeh Lachem* / "this month is for you" (*Shemos* 12:2). 'You, human beings, decide when each month begins,' says Hashem, 'you create and reveal time.'

For this reason, Chazal intuited and received in the Mesorah, that when the Torah says to count "from after Shabbos," it does not mean to start with Hashem's Shabbos, the Seventh Day on which Hashem rested, Hashem's time. It means to start after 'our' day of rest, our time, the day of Pesach, whose exact date was established by human beings.

How do we establish Pesach? Pesach is the 15th day of the month of Nisan, so the actual question is how do we establish the first day of the month. In Temple times this was done with witnesses who came to the high court and testified that they saw the new moon. It was the human eye and the human mind which 'created' or determined the first day, and thus the subsequent days of the month as well.

The lunar cycle is 28 days, however, because of its interplay with the solar cycle within our perspective, it takes approximately 29 and a half days for the new moon to be perceivable. Since the moon is only visible after 29 days, and even then it might not be immediately seen, months can have either 29 or 30 days. This is how the process played out. If, on the 30th day of a month, two witnesses came forward and properly testified that they saw the new moon, then the high court would declare *Mekudash Mekudash* / sanctified, sanctified; and that day would become Rosh Chodesh, the first day of the new month. As a result, the previous month would be retroactively defined as a 29 day month. If no witnesses came forward on the 30th day of the month, then the high court would establish the following day as the first day of the new month, and the previous month would have had 30 days.

Fourteen days later, Pesach would then have fallen on one of two days. The date of Pesach ultimately depended on human perception and the agreement and ruling of the High Court. When we count from Pesach we are counting from 'our time.'

Chazal disagreed that Moshe, a lover of Israel, must have designed the calendar in such a way that a two-day weekend would always automatically descend from Above. They felt that true love is not essentially about giving others gifts without their participation or active receptivity. Rather, real love is like real education; it allows the recipient to value the gift by earning it or co-creating it. Thus, Chazal's response, "Moshe allowed the people to remain in the desert for 40 years!" He allowed the entire community to 'create' their entrance into Eretz Yisrael, to elevate themselves and inhabit the Holy Land by virtue of their own desire. Thus, like the Torah, Eretz Yisrael was given *to us*.

This process was not easy for Klal Yisrael. "Rabba said, 'Conclude from here that a person does not understand the opinion of his teacher until after 40 years'" (*Avodah Zarah*, 5b). It took 40 years for Klal Yisrael to rise to the understanding of Moshe and to truly desire Eretz Yisrael like Moshe did.

RAV YOCHANAN BEN ZAKAI

Who was the sage that responded to the Tzedukim? Rav Yochanan ben Zakai. Nothing is mere coincidence. The name Yochanan Ben Zakai — which in Hebrew means 'Hashem Gives (Y-h Chanan) the son of (ben) Merit (Zakai).' That is, he was an embodiment of the quality of 'meriting' or participating in Hashem's gifts.

Rav Yochanan ben Zakai embodies the worldview of Chazal: Hashem gives us the gift of Torah so that we will toil in it and be *Mechadesh* / creators of new understandings in it. Likewise does Hashem give us time so that we can own it and sanctify it.

Torah and Mitzvos are rooted in a transcendental realm, but Hashem gave them to us, and we should receive them through our merit, with our toil, devotion and exertion. The Torah was given in the third month, as explored earlier, which symbolizes the marriage of Heaven and earth, as well as innovation. This is also the month of the left leg. Together with the right leg of Nisan, we have two feet. With only one foot we can skip and hop, but with two feet we can stand and walk on our own; and this is the ultimate objective of the Torah; to fuse the Heavenly revelation of Mount Sinai with our human capacity to think, innovate and apply the principles of Torah to multitudes of earthly situations.

This kind of giving is true love. And this is the deeper reason why the Torah does not clearly tell us when Matan Torah is, leaving us with the ambiguity of when to start counting. Hashem wants us to become truly intimate with Divinity by participating, discovering, revealing, and co-creating our relationship.

TIME OF THIS ENCOUNTER

Poignantly relevant to their times is the episode with Rav Yochanan ben Zakai and the Tzedukim. Rav Yochanan ben Zakai
had lived through the destruction of the second Beis haMikdash.
During the siege of Yerushalayim, he argued for peace with the
Romans. At some point, he arranged through his students, a secret escape from the city. He was enclosed within a coffin, and the
students pretended that their teacher's body needed to be carried
out of Yerushalayim to be interred. When he had escaped the city,
Rav Yochanan sought out Vespasian, the military commander, and
told him that he would very soon become the new Roman emperor,
and that the Beis haMikdash would soon be destroyed. In return
for this prophetic information, Vespasian granted Rav Yochanan
three wishes. One of Rav Yochanan's requests was the salvation of
the city of Yavneh and its Sages (*Gittin*, 56a-56b). Yavneh became
the cradle of Torah she-b'al-Peh after the destruction of the Beis
haMikdash.

After the destruction of Yerushalayim and the Second Temple
in the year 70 CE, Yavneh became the central residence of Chazal.
The Sanhedrin moved there and established many *Halachos* / laws,
as well as the calendar and the liturgy of Tefilah.

Rav Yochanan lived during the conclusion of the age of prophecy coinciding with the destruction of the first Beis haMikdash,
and helped to launch a new era, with the proliferation of Torah
she-b'al-Peh. The Mishnah was concluded shortly thereafter, and
then began the period of the *Gemara* / Talmud. He knew that with
the ensuing exile from Yerushalayim and the paradigm of 'proph-

ecy-from-Above,' there was a need for Gemara, human participation, toil and innovation/creativity from below. This is the love that Hashem has for us, that we should grow strong, and stand to walk on our own. Hashem wanted us to internalize the Torah and make it ours, so that we could carry it on our journey through exile to the ultimate Redemption.

THE TORAH ITSELF ALLUDES TO ITS TWO LEVELS

Rav Yochanan ben Zakai told the Tzedukim, "One verse says, 'You shall number 50 days,' while the other verse says, 'Seven weeks shall there be complete.' How are these to be reconciled? The latter verse refers to the time when the [first day of the] Festival [of Pesach] falls on Shabbos (thus seven full weeks), while the former refers to the time when the [first day of the] Festival falls on a weekday (and therefore Shavuos will be on the 50th day irrespective of the completion of the final weekly unit)."

Rav Yochanan was telling them, 'There are two ways to count. One way is to count "complete weeks" which by definition concludes with Shabbos, and this is the way Hashem set up time, beyond our participation. But the Torah also alludes to another paradigm, which is "50 days." In this perspective, the 50th day can theoretically fall on any day of the week. Shavuos, like Pesach, can then fall on a weekday, a day which is normally characterized by human toil. In exile, we are currently in an era of *human participation*.' Human participation is the way the Torah will continue to be revealed until the coming of Moshiach, may it be speedily in our days.

In the desert, Moshe hit the rock to bring forth water (water is an allusion to Torah. *Baba Kama*, 82a). Since the destruction of the Beis haMikdash we receive Torah through 'hitting the rock' — through debate and 'colliding' with other perspectives, through creative ingenuity and analysis. When we 'own' the principles that were revealed at Mount Sinai, and align our way of thinking with the Torah, we are able to reveal Chidushim in Torah.

Rav Yochanan ben Zakai is also implying, 'I can show you that within the Torah she-b'Kesav, and within this very Mitzvah of counting time, that Hashem has also given us a Torah she-b'al-Peh; there is Revelation and there is also *participation*.' The Written Torah itself alludes to these two dimensions by enumerating the different perspectives of "seven full weeks' or counting by *Hashem's time*; and "50 days" or counting after Pesach — *our time*.

Essay Two
༃
WHEN AND WHERE WAS THE TORAH GIVEN?

S HAVUOS IS CALLED BY OUR SAGES, "THE TIME OF THE GIVING of the Torah." Yet, nowhere in the Torah itself does it specify the day of the month on which the Torah was given. The date of *Yetzias Mitzrayim* / going out of Egypt is unambiguous. But *Matan Torah* / the Giving of the Torah — arguably the most important event, the crowning moment of all of history — how could it not be specified? Why is the date of Matan Torah not clearly written?

This question pertaining to the realm of time also extends to the realm of space: where was the Torah given?

We know that the Torah was given at "Mount Sinai" but where exactly is Mount Sinai? Up until this day it is not clear where this mountain is. For years many have claimed that it is within the "Sinai Desert" and indeed a certain mountain there has been marked and enshrined as such. However neither the Torah nor Chazal identify the location of Mount Sinai as being in the Sinai Desert (Although, see *Tal Oros*, 1:1). Today, there are archeologists and historians who suggest that the mountain may in fact be in modern day Saudi Arabia.

Why is this mystery so persistent? What does this absence of markers in time and place tell us? Perhaps it is because Torah itself is 'beyond time and space.' The Torah exists *Kadmah* / before Creation (*Pesachim*, 54a), and it is one with the Creator (*Zohar* 1, 60a. "Hashem, Torah and Israel are one," is quoted frequently in *Chassidus* in the name of the Zohar, and it also appears in many sources, such as the *Nefesh haChayim*, in the *Ramchal*. Although it is not actually stated clearly anywhere in the Zohar — see for example, *Zohar* 3, 73a). Unified with the Creator of time and space, the Torah is thus beyond time and space and it connects us to the *Ohr Ein Sof* / the Infinite Light of Hashem beyond all time and space. This is the deeper reason why Matan Torah is not marked as occuring on a specific day nor is the location of Matan Torah pin-pointed. Torah is transcendent, eternal and infinite, and thus relevant at all times and in all places. Torah transcends time and space, yet it also permeates all time and space, as the Torah is the 'blueprint' for the creation of time and space, and the world is thus a *Roshem* / imprint of the Torah.

FORTY NINE IS TIME & SPACE, DIMENSIONALITY; 50 IS BEYOND TIME & SPACE, DIMENSIONLESS

As explored previously, while we are asked to count seven weeks, it also says we need to count 50 days: "And you shall count for yourselves... seven weeks... count 50 days " (*Vayikra*, 23:15-16). As both of these paradigms of counting are to reach Matan Torah on Shavuos, they are connected to two levels of Torah: Torah beyond time and space, and Torah as vested within time and space.

Seven represents the cycles within creation, as in the seven days of the week, this is the world of 'time.' The fullness of seven, seven times seven, is 49, which is the fullness of 'time.' For example, within a seven year cycle, the seventh year is a *Shemitah* / rest of the land, and after seven Shemitahs, 49 years, the full cycle of 'time' is complete. This symbolizes the entirety of the realm of time from a human perspective; anything beyond this would be termed 'timelessness.'

When the Torah says we need to measure, define units, and count 49 days until we get to Shavuos, it is hinting to us how Torah is the foundation of time and space, permeating all measurements and definitions. And when the Torah says, "Count 50 days," it is hinting to the level of Torah which is beyond this world of space-time and dimensionality.

Through counting the 49 days we are moving from the realm of finite, defined digits, to the border between the world of space-time and the world of Infinity (*Ohr haChayim*, Vayikra, 23:15), the realm of 50.

Torah is "ארכה מארץ מדה ורחבה מני־ים" / "Longer than the earth's measure (*Midah*) and wider than the sea (*Yam*)" (*Iyov*, 11:9). The word מדה / *Midah* / measure, has a numerical value of 49 (*Megaleh Amukos*, Parshas Behar. This is in an earlier source as well: *Sefer Rokeach*, Hilchos Pesach, 294. Mem/40, Dalet/4, Hei/5 = 49). The Torah is beyond measure, beyond space-time, connected to the 'limitless' sea; *Yam* in numerical value is 50 (Yud/10, Mem/40 = 50). The Torah is one with the 'Yam,' which is also called *Mayim sh'Ein Lahen Sof* / water which has no end (*Yevamos*, 121a) — as it is one with the Infinite Endless One, the Torah itself is endless.

The Torah is beyond measurement, beyond all numbers, beyond the temporality. Similarly, Klal Yisrael are one with Hashem, and yet are 'counted and measured.' On the other hand, "...The *Mispar* / number of the People of Israel shall be as the sand of the sea, which *cannot* be... counted" (*Hoshea* 2:1). In other words, Klal Yisrael can be counted and are also beyond counting. Because Torah is beyond space-time, it infuses all of space-time.

CREATING TIME

Cycles of time can be divided into two categories: natural cycles and Divine cycles.

The natural cycles of time, such as years and months, are connected to astronomical or agricultural phenomena. Months are inherent within nature; it is an astrological fact that the cycle of the moon is about 29 days. The same is true with years, which is a natural solar cycle of about 365 days. A person lost in the desert can look up at the sky and know approximately what day of the month it is. And just by observing the air temperature or plant life, one can know what phase of the solar year it is.

We also observe a weekly cycle, but there is nothing inherent within nature that dictates a seven day week, or even a week of another number of days. Hashem created weeks. They are the Creator's cycle, so to speak. Weeks have no natural, seasonal or astronomical coordinates. They are a transcendental phenomenon.

There is no Mitzvah to count the seven days of the week such as, "Today is Sunday, today is Monday..." When, in our daily Shacharis service, we say *haYom Yom Rishon baShabbos* / 'Today is the first day of the week,' we are not *making* it the first day, we are merely noting the day in relation to Shabbos; it is part of the Mitzvah to remember Shabbos. Shabbos is already sanctified and established by Hashem; it is Divine time. The manifestation of Shabbos has no connection to any natural phenomena or human participation.

We do, however, need to sanctify months. We are asked by the Torah to take this natural astrological phenomenon and create its contours and imbue it with meaning. We create 'our time.'

Counting the time between Pesach and Shavuos is an even deeper phenomenon. Not only do we sanctify and create time, but we are invited and empowered to create 'weeks' — the Creator's time. Our counting paradoxically creates a construct that is inherently Divine, from Above.

There are also two types of positive Mitzvos. There are Mitzvos that are time-bound, meaning, they have a specific time when they need to be performed, such as blowing the Shofar on Rosh Hashanah or shaking the Lulav on Sukkos. And there are positive Mitzvos that are not time-bound, rather they are applicable at all times, such as the Mitzvah to love your neighbor or love Hashem. It seems very peculiar that the illustrious Ramban writes (on *Kidushin*, 33b) that the counting of the Omer is not a time-bound Mitzvah, even though the Mitzvah is clearly to count from the second day of Pesach until Erev Shavuos.

There are various ways to think about this idea of the Ramban, as explored earlier. One way is that the Mitzvah is not to count time during this period, rather it is to create time. As we are creating time, the Mitzvah is not time-bound, rather, time is bound by the Mitzvah.

Similarly, there was a Mitzvah for the *Beis Din* / high court of ancient Yerushalayim to count seven yearly cycles, towards the *Yovel* / Jubilee, the 50th year. We are the owners of time. What gives us the power to be a 'creator' of time, as the Creator is? It is because we are connected to Matan Torah, which is beyond time and space.

Even though Matan Torah happened in a particular space and at a specific time, the source of Torah is beyond space-time, there is no exact date, time or place. This phenomenon is revealed in our Mitzvah of creating time, we are beyond time and in control as the masters of time. We are now and forever connected to the 50th level, completely free, one with the Timeless Infinite.

Essay Three

🜪

THE NIGHT OF MATAN TORAH:
From Klal to Prat and Back to Klal

O n Shavuos we celebrate the giving of the Torah at Mount Sinai. It is a time when Infinite Divine Intelligence, the Torah and the purpose of Creation was revealed within the finite world of time and space.

When this Higher Intelligence first entered the world, it was an utterly simple seed. The entire Torah was encapsulated within the Aleph, the first letter of the first word revealed at Mount Sinai, the Aleph of the word *Anochi*.

At Mount Sinai there was the revealing of the Ten *Dibros* / Utterances or 'Commandments.' These Ten are the roots of all the Mitzvos in the Torah, and all 613 Commandments can be categorized into ten corresponding groups. (There are 13 *Pesukim* / verses in the Ten Dibros (*Shemos*, 20:2-14. *Devarim*, 5: 6-18). 13 is Echad /one.) However, out of the Ten, *Klal Yisrael* / the People of Israel heard perhaps only the first two of the ten: *Anochi Hashem* / "I am Hashem," and "Do not have any other gods..."

From this perspective, these two are the source of all the commandments. The root of all positive commands is *Anochi* and the root of all negative commands is "Do not have any other gods..."

On another level, perhaps all that the People heard was the first utterance, *Anochi Hashem*. From this perspective, there is a single root of all the Mitzvos; all of Torah is rooted in "I am Hashem." Even deeper, perhaps all that the People heard was the single Aleph of *Anochi*; they heard and absorbed the idea of Aleph, the Oneness of Hashem.

These different options, Aleph, Anochi Hashem, or the first two commandments, can each be called the *Klal* of the Torah, its original 'generality' or unified state. From this original *Klal*, the Torah began to flower into 'many-ness.' In the case of Aleph, the first letter became the first word, which became the first sentence known as the First Commandment, and this expanded into two utterances and then ten. These ten utterances were then articulated as the 613 Mitzvos, then as the thousands of words in the five books of the Chumash, and then as the countless meanings, lessons, applications, complexities and details — Pratim — of Torah wisdom.

This is the ever-expanding movement of the revealing of Torah — from Klal to Prat / from generalities to specifics.

FROM KLAL TO PRATIM

The pattern of the One evolving into the many is found throughout all of creation. The *Klal*, like a seed, sprouts and flowers as Pra-*tim* / diverse expressions of the original package.

Parenthetically, the word כלל / *Klal* is a term used by the *Chokrim* / philosophers. A very similar idea, in the language of the *Mekubalim* / Kabbalists, is often expressed as שורש / *Shoresh* / root. Later in the teachings of the Baal Shem Tov and his students, a very similar idea is expressed as ממוצע / *Memutzah* / intermediary, as it is the intermediary space where the Infinite Formless Source passes through to become a manifest reality. Each of these meanings is slightly different, but for our purposes they can all be implied by the word *Klal*, which we will continue to use.

All organisms, including our own bodies, begin with a single cell. This cell divides innumerably, differentiating according to the vast multitudes of needs and functions. The higher the form of life, the more complex the organism. The movement in Creation is from the *Klali* / singular or simple to the more *Prati* / detailed and complex.

As babies, our lives are very simple and straightforward; we need to eat, drink, sleep, feel the affection of caregivers, and eliminate any discomfort. As we mature, we begin to form more and more complex needs, preferences and opinions.

On a more collective level, the Jewish People began as one person — the first Jew-by-birth being Yitzchak (perhaps the Avos did not have a *Din* / legal designation of *Yisrael*, as they lived before Matan Torah, however they were certainly 'Jewish') — and he had two sons, both being Jewish, Ya'akov and Esav (the latter was a *Yisrael Mumar* / a Jewish heretic, *Kidushin*, 18a), so from one became two. Then Ya'akov had 12 sons, who later evolved into 70 souls as they descended into Egypt (Seventy souls corresponding to the 70 nations of the world). Then at Mount Sinai there were 600,000 souls. Eventually the People of Israel became a diverse group of tribes, each with different characteristics and life-paths.

Creation itself began in utter simplicity: the Torah calls the first day of Creation *Yom Echad* / a 'Day of Oneness.' On subsequent days, this 'oneness' began to unfold itself as 'the many.'

Even Divinity itself appears, from our perspective, to have 'evolved' according to this pattern *Keviyachol* / so-to-speak. That is, prior to the *Tzimtzum* / the Divine Self-contraction, the Infinite Light existed without boundaries, gradations, or attributes. After the *Tzimtzum*, vastly diverse vessels, worlds, and 'levels' of Divinity came into being.

PRATIM OF TORAH

After Mount Sinai, the People of Israel naturally began to fashion Torah-Pratim, because it was too hard to understand or internalize the original Klal. Perhaps the experience of revelation was too overwhelming. Perhaps too much information was packaged in the seed-like words to make sense to the limited human mind.

There are various opinions about what the community actually heard, and were able to internalize, on Mount Sinai. The *Even Ezra* says (commenting on *Shemos*, 20:1) that the people heard and understood each of the Ten Commandments. The Ramban says that all Ten Commandments were heard, and to some extent internalized, by the whole congregation. However, only the first two Commandments were clear to them, and Moshe had to repeat and explain the latter eight (See Shemos, 20:7). Rashi suggests (commenting on Shemos, 19:19. *Makos*, 24a) that only the first two Commandments were directly transmitted to the people, whereas the subsequent eight had to be transmitted through Moshe. The Rambam says they heard the Divine voice and experienced the revelation, but couldn't make any sense out of any of it (*Moreh Nevuchim*, 2:33). Therefore, the majority of these major commentators indicate that the original Klal of the Torah was not understood or internalized by the people. They were able to relate more to the Pratim.

Our Sages discuss this, interpreting the verse, *And they stood under the Mount...* "This teaches us that the Holy One, blessed be He, overturned the mountain upon them like an inverted casket, and said to them, 'If you accept the Torah, good. If not, this will be your burial.' This furnishes a strong protest against the Torah" (*Shabbos*, 88a). In other words, the direct revelation was imposed from Above. One cannot fully internalize information without consciously choosing it or participating in it. Therefore the people had to become creative with the Torah and apply it to the details of their lives.

PRATIM RETURNING TO THE KLAL

This is not the end of the story however. The Gemara continues, "Said Raba, 'Yet, even so, they re-accepted it in the days of

Achashveirosh, for it is written, "They confirmed, and took upon themselves…." They confirmed what they had accepted long before.'" In order to fully internalize the revelation, the community had to re-accept it many centuries later, during the events of the Purim story.

In the era of Purim, the Jewish People had fallen away from the practice of Torah, and the last generation of Prophecy had ended. They were living in exile and anti-Semites had finally decided to wipe them out. This threat stimulated the Jews to band together. When, as one, they re-accepted the Torah, a great salvation occurred. Queen Esther asked that the story of this extraordinary salvation be written as a sacred text, that it be considered part of the Torah, and that a new Yom Tov be created. Her innovations were unprecedented, for what human being can create Divine words or commandments?

However, the power to co-create Torah comes from the Torah itself. Every *Chidush* / authentic innovation in Torah created by human beings throughout history was actually given to Moshe at Mount Sinai: "Even what a proficient pupil is destined to *Mechadesh* / innovate (*Megilah*, 19b), was already said to Moshe at Sinai" (Yerushalmi, *Pe'ah*, 2:4). This seems paradoxical: if it is an innovation, how can it be 'given'? And if the insight was really given on Mount Sinai originally, how is it a Chidush? At Mount Sinai, the Torah was revealed as a Klal, but the Pratim were not yet fully revealed. When we employ our creative process of innovation, and stay true to the original Klal, our innovation can become an actual part of the Divine revelation. With Queen Esther, a new era began; humans and Divine can co-create Torah.

A question is asked: if the Nation of Israel had already accepted the Torah upon themselves, why did Hashem suspend the mountain above their heads and impose the revelation on them? The *Medrash Tanchumah* (Parshas Noach) unpacks this idea, telling us that the people were ready and willing to accept the Written Torah with all the laws that were directly transmitted on Mount Sinai. "All that Hashem utters we will do" — all that *Hashem* utters, but not the later innovations and revelations through the interpretation of the Oral Torah by the Sages. It was only much later, with the story of Purim, that they finally accepted the entire Torah in full, including the oral aspect.

Woven into the fabric of the *Pratim* / many details, is the memory of a *Klal* / an all-inclusive source. Everything and everyone yearns to return to its Klal. We may long for our own childlike simplicity and innocence, or for wholeness, or to be included within the Klal of a group identity. The deeper spiritual instinct behind this yearning is to embrace ourselves and others in non-dual awareness. Ultimately, we seek to bring all of creation back with us to the One. The means to this ultimate accomplishment is the Divine intelligence transmitted through the Torah.

TIKUN

Tikun / repair is to return something to its original wholeness and unity. On Shavuos night, we recite the *Tikun Leil Shavuos* — the inspired compilation of verses from the Five Books, the Prophets, Writings, and the seminal books of Divine inspiration. In this practice, we are not literally 'studying' Torah, rather, we are sweeping through the texts and gathering together the Torah's Pratim into a simple and unified whole; thereby creating wholeness. We thus return the Torah to its source within the Klal of the Aleph, and beyond. By remaining awake all night, immersed in words of Torah, we become highly receptive, and thus able to internalize something of the Klal. We relive the experience of Mount Sinai, each year brings more of the Klal down into the human mind and heart.

DEEPER WHOLENESS

When Avraham, the first person to become a Jew, first encountered the Divine, he heard the words, "I will make you into a great nation" (*Bereishis,* 12:2). Hundreds of years later, when his descendants stood at Mount Sinai, they indeed became a singular nation, "like one person with one heart" (*Mechilta,* Rashi, Shemos, 19:2). However, this unity didn't erase the uniqueness of any individual. The Medrash says that at Mount Sinai each person heard the Divine voice (Klal) speaking as his or her own unique personal voice (Prat).

Similarly, while the first seed of Torah was prior to any differentiation, it did contain the potentiality of all Torah-details. After the process of differentiation, the Pratim of Torah can be gathered into the Klal through *Tikun.* However the Pratim do not then merge back into an undifferentiated state — this wholeness *includes* differentiation. 'Oneness' and 'many-ness', Klal and Pratim, are now simultaneous. This is the difference between the original Klal of Mount Sinai, and the Klal created through the ingathering of Pratim.

Again, we can understand this pattern in our own lives. At first, when we were babies, we had no separate ego — everything was just an extension of our bodies. When we grew, we began to develop an individual ego, an identity separate from everyone else. In a state of spiritual maturity, however, our egos becomes transparent: 'I exist, and so do you.' As an example, in this phase of inclusivity, spouses are able to meet and co-create new babies.

This principle of 'Klal to Prat to the greater Klal of Tikun' is found throughout all of Creation.* The following are examples of this principle as expressed in the three ingredients of Creation: *Olam* / space, *Shanah* / time and *Nefesh* / soul:

---

* The entire process and purpose of creation unfolds in the context of a Klal, Prat, Klal paradigm. Prior to Creation there is, in our terms, only the Divine Klal, the Absolute Unity of Hashem. As this Klal is the Ultimate Klal, it includes all *Peratim* / details, for, "just as Hashem has the potential of infinity (*Bli Gevul* / infinity, or *Ein Sof* / within end), He also contains the potential of finitude (*Koach HaGevul* / potential of finitude)." Prior to the *Tzimtzum* / contraction of the Infinite Light, all that was 'revealed' in the original Klal was Infinity; as finitude was overwhelmed in the presence of Infinity. The Tzimtzum of the Infinite Light allowed for the revealing of finitude, *Pratim* / details, duality, vessels... Eventually, this allowed for the creation of *Yesh* / physical existence, the world of Pratim. Yet, the purpose of the creation of Pratim is that we, human beings, recognize the Oneness of Hashem, and sense how all the Pratim, and even physical existence, are included within the Ultimate Klal of Hashem Echad. In other words, to bring the Pratim (that were never "actualized" in the original Klal) back (in a conscious and revealed manner) to the original Klal. In the language of the Zohar (*Zohar* 2, 25a), "...to know, that there is a supreme ruler, who is the Master of the universe, who created Heaven and earth and all their inhabitants. And this is the Klal, and the end of the Klal is the Prat. To know that it (the Klal) is in the Prat." / למנדע דאית שליטא עלאה, דאיהו רבון עלמא, וברא עלמין כלהו, שמיא וארעא וכל חיליהון. ודא איהו דכלא בכללא. וסופא דכלא בפרט, למנדע ליה בפרט

Ultimate Wholeness in Space:

עד שלא נבחרה ארץ ישראל, היו כל הארצות כשרות לדברות, משנבחרה ארץ ישראל יצאו כל הארצות / "Before the land of Israel was chosen, all of the lands were Kosher for utterances (Divine Prophecy). Once it was chosen, all other lands were excluded" (*Mechilta d'Rebbe Yishmael*, 12:1). This means that before Eretz Yisrael was sanctified, the Kedusha of Eretz Yisrael permeated all space. This is the Klal (R. Yoseph Engel, *Beis haOtzer*, Aleph-Dalet, 12). Then, once Eretz Yisrael was chosen as a Prat, it excluded all other lands.

Eventually, at the *G'mar haTikun* / the final elevation to wholeness of this world, the Kedusha of Eretz Yisrael will again envelope the entire world (Klal), as is well-known, עתידה ארץ ישראל שתתפשט בכל הארצות / "In the future, Eretz Yisrael will spread throughout the entire world." (Although, there is no clear statement as such in Chazal, see, however, *Sifrei*, Devarim beginning with עתידה ירושלים להיות כארץ ישראל וארץ ישראל ככל העולם כולו. *Pesikta Rabbah*, Parshas Shabbos. *Yalkut Shimoni*, Yeshayahu, 503). This demonstrates that the second Klal includes both the first Klal and the Prat; there will still be a specific "Eretz Yisrael" in the future, and yet the Kedusha of Eretz Yisrael will "spread out" to the entire world.

Ultimate Wholeness in Time:

If Adam, who was created on Erev Shabbos, had not eaten from the Tree of Knowledge, it would have been 'Shabbos' for all time (Klal). Because he ate from the Tree of Knowledge, engendering the perception of duality, Adam descended into a binary form of time in which weekdays and Shabbos are separate periods. Since then, humanity experiences Shabbos only once a week (Prat). Yet, eventually, with the G'mar haTikun, every day will be Shabbos, as it will be יום שכולו שבת ומנוחה לחיי העולמים / "a day that will be entirely Shabbos and rest for life everlasting" (*Tamid*, 33b).

Again, the second Klal embraces both the first Klal and the Prat: in the future there will still be a progression of time ("everlasting") and thus there will be a seventh-day Shabbos (Prat), yet the light and rest of Shabbos will entirely permeate every day, as if there is only "a day..." or one day (Klal).

Ultimate Wholeness in Soul:

עד שלא נבחר אהרן היו כל ישראל כשרים לכהונה, משנבחר אהרן יצאו כל ישראל / "Before Aaron was chosen, all of Israel were Kosher for the priesthood (Klal). Once he was chosen, the rest of Israel were excluded (Prat)." Yet, the promise of all of Klal Yisrael was, and is, ואתם תהיו־לי ממלכת כהנים / "and you shall be to Me a kingdom of priests" (*Shemos*, 19:6).

More strikingly, before Matan Torah all people were called Adam (*Tosefos*, Nidda, 70b). As Rav Yoseph Engel points out, before Matan Torah, the idea of *Yisraelis* / Jewishness extended to all nations of the world (*Beis haOtzer*, Aleph-Dalet, 12. R. Shlomo Molcho, in *Sefer haMefuar*, teaches that originally, prior to eating from the Tree of Knowledge, "Just as HaKadosh Baruch Hu is One, there was only One Nation, Klal Yisrael, and no other nations") (Klal). Since Matan Torah there is a Bechira of Klal Yisrael (Prat). Eventually, at the G'mar HaTikun, "Israel will dwell in safety with the wicked of the world... and they will all return to the true faith, and they will not steal and not destroy" / יהיו ישראל יושבין לבטח עם רשעי עכו״ם... ויחזרו כלם לדת האמת ולא יגזלו ולא ישחיתו (Rambam, *Hilchos Melachim*, 12:1).

There will still be Bnei Yisrael (Prat) and the nations of the world, yet the Kedusha of Yisrael will spread out to all people (Klal).

REVELATION, INNOVATION, REVELATION

Now we can appreciate a diagram of the process of revelation. The *Zohar* teaches that there's an underlying unity between the Divine Source, the Torah, and its practitioners (Klal Yisrael) like three links in a chain.

When Hashem reveals to us Divine wisdom from Above, at first we experience overwhelm. However, as we begin to internalize and integrate the experience, our love for the Divine awakens from below, and we seek to reunite with Hashem. With gratitude, we bring our innovations back to their Source, making a Tikun by enfolding our Pratim into the Klal.

In unity with our Source, our innovations are part of Torah. Then the chain of revelation forms a continuous cycle: oneness flows into many-ness, many-iness into Oneness and back into many-ness. This is the flow of light that we can access on the holiday of Shavuos in particular and, in general, every day.

☾

Essay Four

∿

THE ESSENCE OF SHAVUOS:
The Keser of Torah

*T*HERE ARE THREE MAJOR HOLIDAYS IN THE TORAH: Pesach, Sukkos and Shavuos. These are the holidays when there was a Mitzvah to be *Oleh laRegel* / go up to the Beis ha-Mikdash. Unlike Pesach and Sukkos which are both week-long holidays, Shavuos, according to Torah law, is just one day. Why is Shavuos only one day, and what does this teach us about the essence of Shavuos?

Another interesting detail of Shavuos is that in our days, when we are not bringing offerings in the Beis haMikdash, there is very little Torah, and even Rabbinic, law that is unique to this holiday. On the other hand, there are plenty of *Minhagim* / customs adorning this day, such as staying up all night learning, eating dairy foods, and decorating the Shul with flowers or plants. The Arizal speaks about the importance of immersing oneself in the Mikvah on Shavuos, early morning, after staying up all night. The question then arises, how do the Minhagim of the day express the unique essence of Shavuos? To discover this, let us delve deeply into the Minhagim of reciting *Tikun Leil Shavuos*, immersing in a Mikvah, eating dairy on Shavuos, and the fact that Shavuos is Biblically a one day holiday.

While the details of each of the Minhagim will be explored in greater detail in their respective essays, at this juncture they will only be explored in their relationship to the essence of Shavuos itself. This will illuminate both the deeper meanings of the Min- hagim, as well as the uniqueness of the day of Shavuos.

TIKUN LEIL SHAVUOS

The Minhag to stay up all night of Shavuos, learning Torah or reciting the Tikun, goes back more than 1,000 years. (From the source in the Zohar it appears that this practice was and is to be done by select spiri- tually elevated individuals, and not by everyone. Yet, Rav Moshe Machir writes in *Seder haYom* that the *Minhag* / custom is applicable to all. Just a few years after *Seder haYom* was written, it appears that everyone began staying up all night on Shavuos.) The Magen Avraham brings down one reason why we stay up all night. On the night before the giving of the Torah, Klal Yisrael went to sleep; and they slept into the early morning when they were to receive the Torah (*Medrash Rabbah,* Shir haShirim, 1:12). Therefore we create a *Tikun* / repair for their behavior and stay up all night. While this seems straightforward, there is a burning question. How indeed did Klal Yisrael sleep so "peacefully" that night? If they were waiting and counting down the days from when they left Egypt until they were to receive the Torah, how could they sleep at all? Imagine, you have a flight at 6am, and you are very excited about the trip. It is almost certain that you will not be able to easily fall asleep. Even if you do sleep, certainly since there is a chance that you will oversleep and miss the flight, you will set an alarm and excitedly banish sleep from your eyes very early in the morning.

A prevailing custom, based on the practice of the Beis Yoseph, is to recite Tikun throughout the night. Tikun is a compilation of verses, first and last, from the entire Torah, Prophets and writings, also, Mishnah, a counting of the Mitzvos and some readings from the Zohar and Sefer Yetzirah. How is this specifically a Tikun for them sleeping? Besides, would it not make more sense to sit and learn Gemara and Poskim, to get involved in deep Torah learning — which indeed is also a custom, albeit not the Kabbalistic one.

Beyond KARES / Death into KESER / Crown

We learn in the Zohar (Hakdamah, 9a), "Sit my dear friends, sit, and let us innovate a Tikun (ornamentation) for the 'Bride' on this night (of Shavuos). Because anyone who participates with Her on this night will be protected Above and below the entire (coming) year, and will go through the year complete." What does "complete" mean? Says the Arizal, "Know, that anyone who banishes sleep the entire night of Shavuos, and studies Torah the entire night, is guaranteed to live through the year, and no harm will befall them the entire year" (*Sha'ar haKavanos,* D'rushei Chag haShavuos, 1). Somehow, this is a night connected to immortality, and if we stay awake throughout the night and learn Torah we will have a complete year, with no harm.

For certain sins there is a type of 'death from heaven' referred to as *Kares* / cut off. The Arizal teaches that if a person stays up a full night learning Torah, it eliminates *Kares Echad* / one spiritual death sentence (*Sha'ar Ruach haKodesh,* Chap. 3). In fact, from one perspective, during the night that we are awake we need to learn the Torah related to the sins we have committed (*Sha'ar haYichudim,* p. 39a). Either way, on Shavuos night we have the power to undo death, and this we do by connecting to the *Keser* / crown of Torah. *Keser* and *Kares* have the same three letters (*Baal haTurim,* Shemos, 20:14), and by hooking into the level of Keser of Torah we are able to eliminate Kares, along with all death.

Shavuos is the 50th level, similar to the 50th year of *Yovel* / Jubilee, equalling total freedom. On Shavuos we reach the Keser, this 50th level (as will be explored later on). Kares is actually connected to 50. Our Sages tell us that someone who deserves Kares will pass on from this world before the age of 50 (Yerushalmi, *Bikurim* 2:1.Tanya, *Igeres haTeshuva,* 4. Or, between age 50 and 60, *Moed Katan,* 28a).

As mentioned, the realm of Keser represents the *Partzuf* / persona of Divine will and desire, the deepest 'reason' to create within Hashem, as it were. Upon this transcendent persona (namely, *Rosh haLavan* / the Head of Whiteness) the Zohar says, "Its 'eyes' are different; they have no lids." They are lidless eyes because "Keser does not rest nor sleep, and it is the Protector of Israel." This is in contrast to Malchus, the persona of Divine Royalty, the manifest existence of Hashem's Light in this world, whom the Zohar calls, "a beautiful maiden without eyes" / עולימתא שפירתא, ולית לה עיינין (*Zohar* 2, Mishpatim, 95a). Whereas, Keser is always awake and present. In actuality, the way this Divine light is projected via the screen and prism of Malchus there is the possibility of 'sleep' or *Hastara* / Divine concealment.

Sleep is a 'cutting off' from awakeness and a subtle form of 'death.' When we connect to Keser, however, the 'lidless' sleepless eyes, we transcend sleep in all its forms, including death. We erase Kares by being connected to Keser. By staying up all night we forge a connection with the Keser of Torah, the dimension in which the Torah is One with Hashem, a spiritual realm transcendent of sleep and separation.

Speaking about the Keser of Torah and about learning during any night of the year, the Rambam writes, "Even though there is a Mitzvah to learn by day and by night, a person learns *Rov* / most of his Chochmah only by night. Therefore, he who wants to merit to receive the Keser of Torah, should be careful every night, and should not waste even one night on sleep" / אף על פי שמצוה ללמד ביום ובלילה אין אדם למד רב חכמתו אלא בלילה. לפיכך מי שרצה לזכות בכתר התורה יזהר בכל לילותיו ולא יאבד אפלו אחד מהן בשנה (*Hilchos Talmud Torah*, 3:13). In other words, banishing sleep from our eyes on this night connects us to the Keser of Torah (see, *Likutei Sichos*, 34. p. 43). If this is true on all nights of the year, on the night of Shavuos this is even truer. The night of Shavuos is the Keser of the Torah.

The Mitteler Rebbe, Rebbe DovBer, guaranteed that if someone is up the entire night of Shavuos he will merit to receive the Keser of Torah (*Sefer haSichos,* Toras Shalom, p. 3. See also *Ma'amarei Admur haZaken,* Year 5666. p. 367-383). What exactly is the Keser of Torah? And what does it mean that on the night of Shavuos we connect with it?

Here again are the words of the Rambam: "Even though there is a Mitzvah to learn by day and by night, a person learns *Rov* / most of his *Chochmah* / wisdom only by night. Therefore, he who wants to merit receiving the Keser of Torah should be careful every night, and should not waste even one night on sleep." Since the Rambam begins by saying that, "a person learns Rov of his Chochmah by night," and continues, "therefore, if you want to receive the Keser of Torah you should learn Torah by night," it seems clear that Rov Chochmah and Keser of Torah are one and the same.

Also in the words of the Rambam, in order for someone to be considered your main teacher, you must learn the Rov of your Chochmah / wisdom from them (*Hilchos Talmud Torah,* 5:9): ברבו מובהק שלמד ממנו רוב חכמתו / "to one outstanding (main) teacher from whom one has gained the majority of his Chochmah..." This does not seem to be a quantitative statement, meaning, one's primary teacher is the teacher one has learned the most time with. Rather, it is a qualitative statement, one's primary teacher is the teacher that gives him outlook, the way of thinking, the gestalt; an organized and holistic way of perceiving, a perception that is perceived as more than the sum of its parts. Maybe you have spent much more time with one teacher, but the teacher that gives you a way how to think is actually your main teacher.

Keser Torah is the רוב / *Rov* / majority or fullness of Chochmah — the comprehensive and inclusive way of seeing the Torah, and the outlook through which one sees all details of learning.

Our individual, more subjective Keser of Torah is our *Klal*, our general outlook through which we perceive all the details of the Torah that we learn. The objective, universal Klal of Torah is the great principle, the Klal of the entire Torah for all.

On Shavuos we receive this singular Klal of the Torah. And this is the reason, as explored in the previous essay, that Shavuos is a one day festival (Biblically and in Israel today). It is the revelation of the Klal, the 'oneness' of Torah. All other major *Yomim Tovim* / holidays are seven days, representing the fullness, the multiplicity, within creation.

THREE LEVELS OF GADLUS

Let us deepen our understanding of this idea of the Klal that is revealed on Shavuos. The Arizal reveals that there are three levels of *Gadlus* / expansiveness or clarity. On Shavuos we are gifted with *Gadlus Shelishi* / the third and highest level of Gadlus, the Gadlus of Keser. Gadlus Shelishi is something we yearn for during the Pesach Seder, unlike the first two levels that are given to us at that time. With the drinking of the four cups we draw down *Mochin* / awareness of the level of *Binah* / understanding. This is called *Gadlus Rishon* / First Level Gadlus, a type of intellectual clarity of awareness. Later, with the eating of Matzah, we draw down Mochin of *Chochmah* / wisdom or higher intuition, which is *Gadlus*

Sheini / second level Gadlus. This is a type of intuitive intellectual sensitivity, in which one senses the unity and clarity of life.

These levels of expanded mind and open heart come to us on Pesach as a miraculous gift from Above with very little effort on our part. However, as such, we cannot fully integrate them. Pesach represents a quantum leap in our spiritual stature; we are catapulted from the 49th level of impurity to a high level of purity. We simply do not have the vessels at this point to assimilate so much light in a sustainable way. The light bounces off of us, so-to-speak, and as a consequence, we soon descend into a deep level of smallness, leaving us liberated but also lost and confused, as if in a vast desert. This is why, following the brilliant Gadlus of Seder night, "the night that shines brighter than day," many people immediately plummet into *Katnus* / smallness and constricted mind. Many feel a type of high on the Seder night, only to wake up the next morning feeling low again, and maybe even lower, in stark juxtaposition to the Gadlus of the night before. And as we enter the stage of semi-mourning or introspection that characterizes the Sefira period, we begin to yearn for our vessels to receive Gadlus on a level that is even deeper than the night of Pesach. We thus prepare for the night of Shavuos. And the more we yearn to receive the revelation of Torah, and desire to follow its path, the more it will be absorbed and assimilated into our consciousness when we finally receive it.

When Shavuos arrives, we receive Gadlus from the level of Keser in a way that we can actually integrate — in the form of the Torah. This is why, prior to the Gadlus of *Matan Torah* / the giving of the Torah, we have to build vessels to receive and integrate it. We do this through the constrictive effect of judgment on ourselves, while yearning strongly enough in order to make it through all the intense inner-work with courage.

When a person is gifted Gadlus, a new way of thinking flows from higher clarity. When a straw catches fire and flares brightly for a few seconds, however, it then rapidly dies out. The reason why the brilliant Gadlus of Seder night does not last is that one does not yet have the proper vessels to receive and integrate it; the person has not yet worked on himself to create the container for it. Yet, the higher Gadlus of Shavuos comes about through one's hard work, desiring to grow and building up vessels, thus the light permeates and is lasting (*Arvei Nachal*, Shemos).

Throughout the Omer period we build 'vessels' out of the desire to receive this Gadlus, so that when it finally descends it is truly appreciated and assimilated, and not merely taken for granted as just another 'gift' from Above, as on Pesach night. The clarity we receive on the night of Pesach is a gift, a miracle, and so, the very next day we need to count Sefira to begin building the proper vessels so we can draw down this utterly clear *Mochin* / intelligence into our lives and our Midos / personal attributes (Rashash, *Nahar Shalom*, p. 64).

There is a twofold advantage to the third level of Gadlus: a) it is lasting and it permeates our consciousness and being, and b) it is also a much higher/deeper form of Gadlus than the previous two levels, it is Gadlus of Keser. Indeed, it is more lasting and permanent because it is of Keser, a reality that touches on the *Atzmi* / Essential Unchanging.

Again, the first two levels of Gadlus is clarity of mind, of Binah and Chochmah, understanding and wisdom, it is a type of intellectual or subtle intuition, sensing the unity, harmony and cohesiveness of life in general and of your life in particular. A type of intellectual gestalt of seeing the bigger picture, or the fuller and greater picture. A mature *Gadol* / big person is 'continuous' or whole, aligned and inwardly unified with his deepest self. By contrast, a *Katan* / young person is broken or cut, as in *Katua*. An immature person lives from a place of dichotomy, fragmentation, every moment another thing excites them, like a child jumping from one thing to the next without any understanding of the bigger picture, or the cohesiveness of life, or how things are connected, how actions in the present have repercussions in the future and so forth. Experiencing Gadlus of *Mochin* / mind, either Binah or Chochmah, is to experience a type of harmony and intellectual sensitivity of the unity of life, of all life.

Gadlus Shelishi is of another order, it is a Gadlus of Keser. It is the experience of Keser. A crown sits atop the head and symbolically unifies all aspects of the body below. The spiritual realm of Keser represents the Transcendence that maintains all opposites, all the paradoxes of life and existence below it, as will shortly be explained.

THE THREE LEVELS OF GADLUS REVEALED IN HISTORY

These three levels also play out in history, as there are three levels of Gadlus that are and will be revealed in creation.

For the most part *haOlam* / the world is a place of *Helem* / concealment (*Sefer HaBahir*, 10). It is a place of immaturity where, like an undeveloped child, we might not see the interconnectedness of life and the harmony of existence. The world seems to function from a place of Katnus; random events seem to occur, people are separated into 'us and them,' and there is a general lack of integrity between soul, mind and body.

This is the way of the world when it is in a Katnus state. Historically, within the realm of *Z'man* / time, Gadlus Rishon (Mochin of Binah) is revealed through the miracles and wonders that Hashem performs in this world. This characterized the period of the first *Beis haMikdash* / Holy Temple (Ramchal, *Sefer haKlalim*, printed in the back of *Da'as Tevunos*, p. 272). During that era, prophecy and open revelations of Divinity abounded. However, they were only revealed to prophets and children (students) of prophets, and those privy to be in or near the Beis haMikdash to witness the daily miracles that occurred there. These revelations and miracles were concealed from those who were neither prophets nor aspiring prophets, or those who lived at great distances from the Beis haMikdash.

Gadlus Sheini, a higher/deeper, more inclusive and more lasting Gadlus will be fully revealed in the times of Moshiach, when, "the entire world will be filled with the knowledge of Hashem" (*Yeshayahu*, 11:15). Then, we will no longer need miracles to show us that there is a Master of this seeming 'castle in flames,' in the language of the Medrash (*Medrash Rabbah,* Bereishis, 39:1). The whole world will then see, "All the flesh together will see the *Kevod* / glory of Hashem" (*Yeshayahu*, 55:8).

The word *Nes* / miracle, also means 'to lift up' high, as today we sometimes need a miraculous event to lift our consciousness and clearly show us and the world around us that Hashem's presence is here. There will come a time when the physical world, the "flesh," will reveal Hashem's presence and there will no longer be any need for special miracles; all of life itself will be seen as a miracle, all things pointing to their Creator.

Beyond this is the Mochin of Keser, the highest, deepest, fully inclusive and everlasting Galdus Shelishi. This is the way the world existed prior to the eating from the Tree of Knowledge, duality, dissension and fragmentation. The world itself will be seen as immortal and perfect, not only pointing to the Creator, but One with the Creator. This absolute clarity is a knowing that is beyond knowledge.

Gadlus Shelishi will be collectively experienced in the time of *Techiyas haMeisim* / the resurrection of the dead. The world of resurrection is the world of Immortality, embracing all of physicality (the body) and living with it for eternity (*Emunos veDeyos*, Ma'amar 7:5. Ra'avad, *Hilchos Teshuvah*, 8:2. Ramban *Sha'ar haG'mul*. Rikanti, Bereishis. *Derashos haRan*, Derush 5. Other Rishonim argue that even after the Techiyah there will be death. *Chovos haLevavos*, Sha'ar 4:4. Rambam *Igeres Techiyas haMesim*, 4. Hilchos Teshuvah 8:2. *Moreh Nevuchim*, 2:27. *Kuzari*, Ma'amar 1:115. *Sefer haIkarim*, Ma'amar 4: 30-33).

In human thinking, time generally seems to flow from the past to the present and then to the future. This division of time, a past 'separated' from the future, is a byproduct of our eating from the Tree of Knowledge of duality. In the Tree of Life consciousness, however, the experience is the reality of unity, all of 'time' occurs simultaneously, as a single presence. When the world eventually attains a full Tikun, when each individual soul has become perfect and whole again, returned to its root in the unified body of primordial Adam, time will be unified as well. At that point the great resurrection of the dead will manifest. This will not simply mean that our souls will inhabit physical forms once again. Rather, since time will reach a point of perfect unification, all of our 'past,' including our bodies, will become present in the here and now.

We live in a universe of three-dimensional space, and a fourth dimension which is time. Each of these dimensions currently exists in a paradigm of separation. In the dimension of time, the 'past' only exists as a memory. The dimension of time also seems to be separate from space. In a unified reality this fourth dimension will be seamlessly manifest within the three dimensions of space. There will thus be a total conservation of energy, and everything of the 'past' will be manifest in the present. There will no longer be a seperate past, for everything will exist within the eternal unified moment. As a result, the bodies of the 'past' will resurrect and live again in the present.

This is life in Gadlus Shelishi, the Gadlus of Keser, in which everything is unified, where the apparent separation of bodies, and the distinction between the body and the soul, no longer assert themselves. This is a total resolution of all polarities and paradoxes, and harmony of body and soul, spirit and matter, spirituality and physicality.

On a microcosmic level, on the night of Shavuos, we receive this level of Gadlus Shelishi. Appropriately, Shavuos is connected to immortality. "Know, that anyone who banishes sleep the entire night of Shavuos, and studies Torah the entire night, is guaranteed to live through the year, and no harm will befall them the entire year" (*Sha'ar haKavanos,* D'rushei Chag haShavuos, 1). Indeed, at Mount Sinai, when we received the Torah we experienced Techiyas haMeisim; our souls had left our bodies and were returned with the *Tal Techiyah* / dew of resurrection (*Shabbos,* 88b). It was only due to the sin of the golden calf that the first *Luchos* / Tablets, the Luchos of Freedom from the angel of death (*Medrash Rabbah,* Shemos, 41), were shattered and we entered again into the world of duality. This state persisted until the time of the first Beis haMikdash, at which point we witnessed Gadlus Rishon. G-d willing, may it arrive speedily in our days, we will experience Gadlus Sheini, with the coming of Moshiach, and Gadlus Shelishi, with the resurrection of all the dead.

EXPERIENTIALLY: THE THREE LEVELS OF GADLUS

Above are described the levels of Gadlus as expressed and experienced within the realm of *Z'man* / time. It is vital that they are also expressed and experienced within the realm of *Nefesh* / soul known as consciousness.

As mentioned, on the night of Pesach, while drinking the four cups of wine, we receive *Gadlus Rishon* / first-level Gadlus, which is the 'great expansion' of *Binah* / understanding, a type of higher intellectual clarity. After the second cup, when we eat Matzah, we draw down *Gadlus Sheini* / second-level Gadlus, which is the 'great expansion' of *Chochmah* / intuitive wisdom. This is a profound intuitive clarity and transparency in which one senses the unity of life.

Binah-level clarity is different than Chochmah-level clarity. The Gadlus of Binah is an intellectual sense that you are doing what you are supposed to be doing and that your life makes sense. The Gadlus of Chochmah is a more intimate and intuitive clarity, a subtler but higher sense that is all perfect and exactly as Hashem wants it to be.

By eating the Matzah we are lifted into this intuitive clarity, which in turn catapults us into a place of freedom and openness. In this deep state, there is a sense of *Deveikus* / oneness with Hashem and unity with your deeper self; you have an absolute clarity regarding who you really are and how you should live your life. This is a taste of redemption.

On Shavuos, we are gifted the highest level, the Gadlus of Keser. Keser is the ultimate clarity of perfect *Emunah* / faith in Hashem. Opposites are unified into a seamless harmony; paradox is tolerated, maintained and made whole.

In the experience of Gadlus of Keser, your entire purpose of being, why you're born and why you are living, is revealed to you. Not only do you 'understand' the entire context of your life; why you have these parents, these siblings, this body, born into this century, in a particular country — but it also makes sense, and you experience the *Ta'anug* / bliss of this awareness. The pleasure and relish of your Avodah comes from Keser. This is not only a Gadlus of the mind, a knowing of the unity/harmony of Creation and of your own life story, but is also the feeling of Ta'anug in this awareness of Keser.

You know and sense why you are here, it feels right, and you know exactly what you need to do in your life. There is absolute clarity. This is the Gadlus of Keser. In the language of the Arizal, the attribute of Tiferes, which can also refer to Klal Yisrael, is unified with and receiving directly from Keser. It is where the level of Yechidah (Keser) is drawn down, and thus Tiferes (ZA) is elevated to Keser (There is a drawing down of the Lamed/Mem of Tzelem, which is *Mochin* / intelligence of *Makifim* / surrounding [Keser] light).

On Shavuos we receive Gadlus on a much deeper/higher, transformative, integrated and compassionate way. At Matan Torah, Hashem appeared to Klal Yisrael as an "old man filled with compassion," says the Medrash (As *Rashi* brings down, Shemos, 20:2). The image of an 'old man' refers to the higher level of Keser, which is called *Atik* / literally *ancient*, but meaning an eternal detachment or timeless transcendence. (Incidentally, according to the Zohar, 50 is connected to זקנה / old age (*Tikunei Zohar*, Tikun 21. *Meorei Ohr*, Os Zayin, 34). And 50 is the day of Matan Torah, where The זקן / old man revealed the Keser of Torah to us. This is in contrast (*Ya'ir Nesiv*, on Meorei Ohr Ibid. *Pirush Hagra* on Tikunei Zohar) to the Mishnah (*Avos*, 5:22), where the age sixty is connected to זקנה. See, the Rebbe, *Sichos Kodesh*, Tav/Shin/Mem, 3, Ekev.)

The Mishnah says, "On Shavuos there is a judgment on the fruits of the tree" / בעצרת על פירות האילן (*Rosh Hashanah*, 16a). Fruit is a luxury, meaning a manifestation of *Ta'anug* / pleasure and desire. Inwardly, the fruit of Shavuos is the Ta'anug of Keser-awareness.

On the night of Shavuos, as we read the Tikun and immerse in the Mikvah, then later listen to and receive the *Aseres haDibros* / Ten Commandments (the Keser of the entire Torah), we are internalizing the timeless clarity of the Sefirah of Keser. We glimpse the Gadlus Shelishi that will be collectively experienced in the times of *Techiyas haMeisim* / the resurrection of the dead. At Matan Torah, Klal Yisrael experienced death and then *Techiyah* / revival (*Shabbos*, 88b. *Medrash Rabbah*, Shir haShirim, 6). Since this experience is 'imprinted' in our yearly cycle, we are able to tap into this revival each year, along with its cause, the Gadlus Shelishi, Atik of Keser.

READING THE LETTERS OF THE TORAH /
THE KESER OF THE TORAH

As mentioned, the Zohar teaches that on Shavuos night we should be "involved in Torah, from [Chumash] to the Prophets, from the Prophets to the Writings, and to the teachings on the verses and the secrets of the Torah." It appears that the main Torah that we need to study on Shavuos night is *Torah she-b'Kesav* / written Torah, and just the very general ideas in it — reading just the first three and final three Pesukim from each Parsha and book in Tanach (Although, *Zohar* (Emor 3, p. 97b) suggests that the main learning at night should be *Torah she-b'al-Peh* / Oral Torah, and the Alter Rebbe in Shulchan Aruch also rules that the *Ikar* / main learning on Shavuos night should be Torah she-b'al-Peh. The Mitteler Rebbe explains (*Sefer haMa'amarim*, Shavuos, p. 326), that a person should recite the Tikun, meaning the Torah she-b'Kesav aspects of the Torah, prior to *Chatzos* / midnight. Then they should go to the Mikvah, and then, after Chatzos, learn the Torah she-b'al-Peh). The Arizal, in *Sha'ar haKavanos*, teaches, "In order to draw down the Keser... begin by reading Bereishis... and from there on, read the three beginning verses and three end verses of every Parshah... then the Prophets in the same manner... until the end of Chabakuk, and then the rest of the night the secrets of the Torah and the Zohar." In other words, we need to sweep through and sample all of Tanach — and the inner intention is to reconnect to the Klal, the Keser.

A fundamental difference between Torah she-b'Kesav and Torah she-b'al-Peh is that in she-b'Kesav, the letters themselves are important and essential, whereas as in she-b'al-Peh, the written <u>words are not </u>as essential as the ideas.*

* Even adding or subtracting one letter, "can destroy the entire world" / מחריב את כל העולם כולו (*Eiruvin,* 13a). And for this reason, the *Sofrim* / sages would count each letter of the Torah (*Kiddushin,* 30a). However, with regards to Torah she-b'al-Peh, Rav Yochanan rules, "those who *write down* Halacha are considered like those who burn the Torah" / כותבי הלכות כשורף התורה (*Temurah,* 14b), as *Rashi* writes, דתורה שבעל פה היא / since it is the *oral part* of Torah. Moreover, it appears that even during the time period of the Gemara, the oral aspect of Torah was (mostly) oral. (Indeed, Rav Yochanan, who posited the above, was in fact considered an Amora, and still ruled as such.) The Ta'anaim (classically known as the sages of the Mishnah), who would record to memory the Mishnah, the main body of the oral tradition, would often be called upon to confirm or settle disputes regarding the correct version of a Mishnah, even during the times of the *Amaraim* / sages of the Gemara and maybe even later. The Gemara mentions דווקני / specific precision with regards to the written Torah or financial documents (*Menachos,* 29b. *Avodah Zarah,* 10a), but not with regards to the 'text' of the Mishnah (as perhaps the Mishnah was (mostly) oral during that time); and for this reason the Gemara mentions דווקני with regards to the sages themselves, the oral tradition (*Yevamos,* 43a). Indeed, when there was a doubt in terms of the correct version of a Mishnah, the Amaraim would say, "let us ask the *Tanah*" / שיילינהו לתנאי (*Niddah,* 43b. *Baba Metziyah,* 34a, although see *Rashi* ad loc). For this reason, being an oral tradition and transmission, many times when the Amaraim were not sure about a precise version of a Mishnah, it was because of the phonetic oral nature of the transmission. For example (*Avodah Zarah,* 2a), חד תני אידיהן וחד תני עידיהן / "One teaches the term meaning *Eideihen* / their festivals (spelled with an Aleph as the first letter) and one teaches *Eideihen* / their witnesses (with an Ayin as the first letter)." Clearly, the issue is phonetic. Or (*Eiruvin,* 53a), חד תני מעברין וחד תני מאברין / "One taught that the term in the Mishnah is Me'abberin (with the letter Ayin (as in a pregnant woman)), and one taught that the term in the Mishnah is Me'avverin (with the letter Aleph (as in a limb))."

In fact, with regards to she-b'Kesav, a person fulfills the Mitzvah of learning Torah just by reading the words, even if with minimal to no understanding. Whereas, in she-b'al-Peh a person only fulfils the Mitzvah when they understand what they are learning.

Reading the words of Torah quickly, much like a scanning of the letters, is a type of learning connected to the she-b'Kesav; and actually, this is how most of Shavuos night is spent in she-b'Kesav, reading Tanach. This type of learning Torah is not a 'left brain' activity. Instead of delving deeply into the meaning of the words, we are connecting more with the words themselves.

In traditional Kabbalistic sources this level is called Keser. In Chassidic language this is called connecting to the *Osyos haTorah* / letters of the Torah. On Shavuos night we need to recite the Osyos haTorah (Rebbe Rayatz, *Sefer Hasichos,* 5700, p. 113) and connect with the Klal, that being the letters of Tanach, the Keser.

By sweeping through the Torah she-b'Kesav and then the Mishnah, which is the basic foundation (Keser or Klal) of Torah she-b'al-Peh, we connect to the level of Keser and gather all the Pratim of the Torah into the Klal (as explained in the previous essay). This unifies the she-b'al-Peh with the she-b'Kesav (*Tikunei Zohar,* Tikun 19. p. 39b) and draws it all back into Keser.

This is the *Avodah* / spiritual work of the night of Shavuos; reaching and tapping into the Keser of Torah, the Keser of all Creation, the Keser of our own consciousness — and thus resurrecting ourselves and eradicating *Kares* / spiritual death. Ultimately, this process will eradicate the very idea of death itself.

TIKUN ON THE NIGHT OF SHAVUOS

When Divine Intelligence first entered the world through the revelation of Matan Torah, it was an utterly simple seed, the Klal and Keser of Torah. The entire Torah was encapsulated within the Aleph, the first letter of the first word revealed at Mount Sinai. For this reason, Rebbe Mendel of Rimanov teaches that at Mount Sinai, Klal Yisrael heard just the *Aleph* / One in (the word) *Anochi*" (*Zera Kodesh*, Shavuos, p. 40).

From this original Klal, the Torah began to flower into 'many-ness.' The first word became the first sentence, known as the first Commandment, which expanded into two sentences and then ten. These ten sentences were then articulated as the 613 Mitzvos and the 620 letters of the *Eser Dibros* / Ten Utterances that Create the world. Then it expanded into the thousands of words in the five books of the Chumash, and then into the literally countless meanings, lessons, applications, and complex *Pratim* / details of Torah wisdom which permeates all of life in the entire universe.

The Aleph of *Anochi* is thus reflected everywhere and in every phenomenon, as it refracts through trillions of trillions of combinations, vibrations, languages, manifestations of energy and articulations of matter. "Hashem looked into the Torah and created the world" (*Medrash Rabbah*, Bereishis, 1:1). "The world is a *Roshem* / an imprint of the Torah, and the Torah is a Roshem of *Elokus* / Divinity" (Shaloh, *Shavuos*, Perek Torah Ohr, 34).

On Shavuos Night when we recite Tikun we are not literally 'studying' Torah. Rather, we are sweeping through the texts to gather together the Pratim into a Klal and return the Torah to its source, its Keser. What's more, by remaining awake all night, immersed in words of Torah, we become highly receptive and internalize something of the Klal. As we thus re-live the experience of Mount Sinai each year, we bring more of the Klal down into the human mind and heart. This is the reason we stay awake on this night.

The ultimate Klal of Torah is beyond the Klal of its expression; it is the silence of the Aleph, beyond the letter Aleph. And yet, as a Klal, it embraces all of the letters and expressions as well. In order to reach this silence of Keser that both transcends and embraces all expression, we need to enter a place within ourselves that is beyond the left-hemisphere, beyond the rational and analytical functions of the brain. 'Sweeping,' or rapidly reciting texts, helps to facilitate this.

WHITE FIRE TORAH: THE INFINITE SOURCE OF TORAH

In actuality, the ultimate Keser, Klal, and source of Torah is Hashem alone. Thus, each Shavuos night, at the moment right before the reading of the Ten Commandments (the expression of the Keser of Mitzvos and the Written and Oral Torah) — and just as the Aleph of *Anochi* is being pronounced — we receive a connection to Hashem, the very Source of Creation.

Once, a troubled young man came to Reb Zusha and told him that his father had passed away recently and was coming to him nightly in disturbing dreams. His father would tell him in the dreams to leave the path of Torah and Mitzvos, Heaven forbid. He was greatly disturbed by these dreams and asked Reb Zusha to help him interpret their meaning. Reb Zusha answered him that there was certainly a crucifix buried near his father's grave, and when he would go dig it up and remove it, the dreams would subside. That is exactly what happened. Sometime later, this story reached the Gra, the Vilna Gaon, who commented: "The fact that Reb Zusha told the person to remove the symbol from the vicinity of the grave is no wonder, as this is alluded to in the Talmud Yerushalmi (Although where it is in the Yerushalmi is uncertain. The Rebbe, *Igros Kodesh*, 11, p. 269). "The wonder," continued the Gra, "is that Reb Zusha knew the Yerushalmi." When the Gra's comment was repeated to Reb Zusha, he said, "Honestly, I have not seen the Yerushalmi, but I did see the idea in the same Source where the (sages of the) Yerushalmi saw it."

Because Reb Zusha was in a constant state of *Deveikus* / living unity with Hashem, the Source, Klal and Ultimate Keser of Torah, he therefore knew Torah globally, from Above and within.

The Torah was given to us as "black fire upon white fire." Within the Torah scroll itself, the black fire is the Torah that is revealed to us, the actual letters, while the white fire is the empty space that surrounds and fills the letters. Symbolically, the black fire (the letter) emerges from the white fire (the empty space). Similarly, our observable world of duality, the *Alma d'Piruda* / world of separation, was created and emerges from *Ein Sof* / the Infinite One, similar to the black defined fire of the Torah that originates in the White Infinite Source of Torah.

The actual words of the Yerushalmi, mentioned by the Gra in the above story are of the articulated 'black fire' of the Torah, yet, the source of the black fire is the infinite 'white fire' of Torah. In the white fire, we can perceive beyond language how every word in the Torah is a Name of Hashem, and deeper, that the entire Torah is one vast Name of Hashem, as the Zohar (2, Yisro, 87a. Zohar, Parshas Shemini in the beginning) teaches.

The white fire, as the Keser, embraces all its expressions. Since Reb Zusha was *Davuk* / unified with the white fire of Torah, and with the Giver of the Torah, he was intuitively able to derive details of the black fire from the standpoint of the 'white fire.'

When we banish sleep from our eyes and are involved all night with learning and reading Torah, our rational brain tires and relaxes; the dualistic apparatus of the mind becomes cloudy. In this state, we are able to slip into connection with the Gadlus of Keser, beyond the duality and detail of the black fire. If we were to fall asleep, much like Klal Yisrael did intentionally on the night of Matan Torah, we might experience *Ayin* / no-thingness or emptiness, but be unable to consciously connect with the ultimate Keser, which includes both the *Yesh* / existence and *Ayin* / non-existence simultaneously. When we stay up and experience some physical and mental tiredness, we are, in a certain way, awake and slightly asleep at the same time. We are thus more able to encompass both the 'awakeness' of Yesh and the 'sleep' of Ayin, thereby connecting with the ultimate Klal and Keser of Torah which embraces all states.

EATING WHITE FOODS / MILK ON SHAVUOS

The earliest source for eating milk products on Shavuos is from the *Kol-Bo*, which is a book attributed to the French scholar, Rav

Aharon of Lunel (1280-1330). He writes that it is a custom to eat 'honey and milk' on the first day of Shavuos, since the Torah is likened to "milk and honey" (This is also the reason offered in *Seder Hayom*, from R. Moshe Machir). A few years later, writing in the late 1300's, Rav Yaakov ben Moshe Mulin (c. 1365-1427) known as the Maharil, mentions the custom to eat and drink milk products, but does not mention honey. Ever since then, the common custom among all Jews is to eat some dairy on Shavuos. There are many reasons offered; in the words of the Alter Rebbe, "There is a *Minhag* / custom to eat dairy foods on the first day of Shavuos, and 'a custom of Israel is Torah.' Many reasons are given" (*Shulchan Aruch haRav*, Orach Chayim, 494:16).*

---

* This is stated in a very peculiar sequence. Seemingly, it should have said, "There is a custom to eat dairy, and many reasons are offered; a custom of Israel is Torah." Furthermore, the Alter Rebbe does not offer even one reason? It could be argued that the Alter Rebbe means to say that the 'reason' it is a custom of Israel, and the reason that it is Torah, is precisely because "many reasons have been given." Since many reasons have been offered, this shows that it is a strong custom and thus qualifies as Torah. And the Alter Rebbe's *reason* to eat dairy on Shavuos is simply because it is a *Minhag Yisrael* / custom of Israel (and not because of any other reason). Among the actual reasons offered, besides those mentioned above:

a. The Torah was given on Shabbos, and it was not possible for Klal Yisrael to Kasher their non-Kosher utensils for cooking meat. Also, Shechitah is prohibited on Shabbos. (*Mishnah Berurah* 494: 12, yet, see *Likutei Sichos* 8, Naso).

b. One of the names of Mount Sinai is 'Mount Gavnunim' (*Medrash Rabba*, Bamidbar, 1:8), and so we eat *Gevinah* / cheese (R. Shimshon Astropoliya).

c. The numerical value of the word *Chalav* / milk is 40, and thus we drink milk to commemorate the 40 days Moshe was on the mountain receiving the Torah. Indeed, the weight of the first Luchos were 40 Se'ah (*Yerushalmi, Ta'anis,* 5:5).

d. White milk represents Chesed (*Rikanti*, Mishpatim, 23:19), and the Torah is called a Torah of Chesed (*Bnei Yissaschar*, Sivan).

e. Milk is pure Chesed, and no knife or even teeth (both connected to Gevurah and Din) are needed to prepare it for digestion, unlike meat which demands a

In this context, milk, a 'white' sustenance (see *Magen Avraham*, Shulchan Aruch, Orach Chayim, 494 regarding white milk being Chesed, and how red 'blood (Gevurah), turns into milk (Chesed). 'Blood turns into milk' is the opinion of Rebbe Meir (*Niddah* 9a).), is clearly related to the 'white fire' of Torah that is revealed on Shavuos.

Our Sages (*Mechilta*, Beshalach, 15:3. Yisro, 20:2) tell us that at the Giving of the Torah, Hashem appeared to Klal Yisrael as an old man filled with compassion. As Rashi brings down (*Shemos*, 20:2), "at *Yetzias Mitzrayim* / the going out of Egypt, Hashem appeared to them as a young man, and at the giving of the Torah like an old man." In the language of the Arizal, "He appeared to them as an old man whose beard is *white*." This 'white' beard, the Arizal connects to the idea of Keser (third level Gadlus), which is also called *the White Head* or *the White Beard*.

As we are connecting to the white fire of Torah, we endeavor to take hair cuts on Erev Shavuos, as when we cut our hair, we are revealing our 'white' scalp, and on Shavuos we eat white milk-based foods.

---

knife to cut it and teeth to chew it. On the day the Torah was given we're like Adam and Chavah in the Garden of Eden, prior to eating from the Tree of Knowledge. In that idyllic pristine state we were like small children and did not digest meat. Similarly, today, we eat dairy on Shavuos (*Derashos Chasam Sofer*, Shavuos).

f. In addition to meat we eat dairy, implying two separate meals or dishes, to commemorate the *Shtei haLechem* / two loaves that were brought on Shavuos (*Machtzis haShekel*, 494:7).

g. These two meals correspond to the two *Luchos* / Tablets.

h. These two meals represent the *Katnus* / infancy that comes before the true *Gadlus* / maturity, which we receive on Shavuos (R. Pinchas of Koritz).

MIKVAH SHAVUOS MORNING

All of the above alludes to why it is so important to immerse in a Mikvah after a full night of being awake and learning Torah (*Zohar* 3, 98a. One immerses just before *Alos haShachar* / dawn. *Pri Eitz Chayim,* Sha'ar Chag haShavuos, 1. *Avodas haKodesh* [Chida]. *Morah b'Etzbah* 8:225. This is also the Chabad custom). Immersing in a Mikvah, being utterly submerged in water, we shed our finitude, as we are ceasing to breathe and thus stop, as it were, being. We become 'infinite.' Our existence is not 'tolerated' or supported underwater, and we experience a Keser, a transcendence of our existence (The level of Ayin within the highest level of Keser maintains Yesh and Ayin simultaneously). This occurs every time we immerse in a Mikvah. However, the Arizal teaches that the Mikvah immersion on Shavuos morning is particularly connected to the *Ohr* / light of Keser. When you dip in the Mikvah on this night / early morning, he says, you need to have the intention that you are immersing in the higher Mikvah, which is Keser. (To do this he recommends visualizing the four letters of the Name Hashem, Yud-Hei-Vav-Hei (perhaps each letter imprinted on one of the four walls of the Mikvah), with the vowel Kamatz beneath each letter. Kamatz corresponds to Keser.)

Lack of sleep is the *Bechinah* / level of Ayin (Keser) and immersing underwater is an even stronger revelation of this. The fullest revelation of the reality of Keser, however, occurs with the reading of the *Eser Dibros* / ten *speakings* or commandments, the tenth Sefirah or Keser of Torah. Then, the final entry and assimilation of Keser into our consciousness is with the recital of 'Keser' in the Kedusha prayer of the Musaf service, which follows the reading of the Torah. This is why it is brought down in the name of the Baal Shem Tov (*Siddur R. Shabtai. Baal Shem al haTorah,* Shavuos, 2) that we should try not to speak any trivial or wasteful words from when we complete the *Tikun Leil Shavuos* until after the "Keser" of Musaf. This helps us hold our Kavanah on Keser from the night until the point when the *Ohr haKeser* has wholly descended.

A ONE-DAY HOLIDAY

All the above helps us understand why Shavuos is only a one day holiday, in contrast to the other major holidays such as Pesach and Sukkos. The Zohar (3, 96a) asks why Pesach and Sukkos are seven days, while Shavuos is one day, and explains it is because Klal Yisrael is a *Goy Echad* / "singular nation" (*Shmuel* 2, 7:23) which is Klal Yisrael's greatest praise. And the Torah is also 'one'; it is called the Tree of Life, the Tree "in the middle of the Garden" that unifies creation into one. The Torah is the Torah of the One, and is itself 'one,' and given over to people who are 'one.' Thus, Shavuos is one day.

WHY TWO DAYS OF SHAVUOS IN THE DIASPORA?

Understanding that Shavuos is the Keser within time helps us to see why Shavuos is a one day Yom Tov, and in the Diaspora a two day Yom Tov. Let us look a little deeper.

According to the order of events, Klal Israel left Egypt on a Thursday, and 50 days later was Shabbos: "All (sages) agree that the Torah was given on Shabbos" (*Shabbos*, 86b). However, this requires investigation. If they left on a Thursday, then 49 days later would again be Thursday, and the 50th day would be Friday, not Shabbos! This question was raised by the Magen Avraham (*Orach Chayim*, 494:1), and one reason he brings for this seeming anomaly, is that there is an allusion to the second day of Yom Tov, which is in fact the 51st day.

The second day of Shavuos is a perplexing phenomenon. The reason why there are two days of Yom Tov in the diaspora is due to doubt, as we will now explain. Holidays such as Pesach and Sukkos always begin on the 15th day of their month. How do we know when the 15th will be? Today we have calendars. However, originally the 15th was calculated based on the first of the month, which was established by means of witnesses. When two eligible witnesses came to the high court in *Yerushalayim* / Jerusalem and testified that they had seen the new moon, the court would rule that the month had begun.

A cycle of the moon is 28 days, however, because of the concurrent solar cycle, it takes approximately 29.5 days for the new moon to be revealed to the eye. Since the new moon can be seen only after that minimum amount of time, a month sometimes has 29 days and sometimes 30 days. If on the 30th day of the month two witnesses came forward and testified that they saw the new moon, then that day would become the first day of the new month, and the previous month would be defined as a 29 day month. If no witnesses had come forward on the 30th day of the month, then the high court would establish the following day as the first day of the new month and the previous month would have contained 30 days.

Once the first day of the month was established, messengers would be sent out to notify Klal Yisrael when Rosh Chodesh was. In those times, there were no reliable means of communication other than travelling by foot or by animal, and for those who lived further than a 15 day journey from Yerushalayim, the timing of the

15th day would be uncertain. Pesach must begin on the 15th day of Nissan. Since the distant community could not have been informed that the previous month was only 29 days, the day they might assume to be the 15th, based on their own observations of the moon, could in fact be the 14th. The Sages ruled that such a community should celebrate Pesach on both days: the day they assumed to be the 15th and the day they assumed to be the 16th of the month. One of the two would have been the actual day of Pesach. As for the inevitable outcome of celebrating one of the two days of Pesach on the wrong day, a *Safek* / doubt regarding a *Mitzvah d'Oraysa* / Torah-based Mitzvah should be approached with stringency; it is more important to celebrate Yom Tov on the 'wrong day' than to not celebrate it on the right day.

This is the root reason that Holidays are observed for two days in locations outside the Land of Israel, where it would take longer than 15 days for messengers to arrive. Today we continue this practice, since this was the custom of our ancestors.

Shavuos was always 50 days from Pesach; it was never related to a calendar day, but derived from Pesach. The question then stands out: why should there be two days of Shavuos? There was no Jewish community in the ancient world that was more than a 50 day travel from Yerushalayim. Shavuos should seemingly be a one day holiday. However, the Rambam (*Hilchos Kidush HaChodesh*, 3:12) writes that we keep two days of Shavuos, כדי שלא לחלק במועדות / "because we do not want to differentiate Holidays" and make special exceptions with the Festivals.*

---

* The grandson of the Nodah beYehudah allowed giving a *Get* / bill of divorce on the second day of Shavuos to prevent an Agunah issue — an act that is prohibited on Yom Tov. Rav Shlomo Kluger argued against this position. The Chasam

Despite our celebration of two days in the Diaspora, Shavuos is *essentially* one long day. Shavuos is the Keser, the great Klal, the Aleph, the Torah of the Tree of Life, of Oneness, the highest/deepest level of Gadlus. Matan Torah is a revelation of *Anochi Hashem*, the Oneness of Hashem that is revealed to the people of Unity, the people of Oneness, on a singular day in a unity of time.

THE NIGHT BEFORE MATAN TORAH:
Why Did They Sleep, and Why Do We Not?

We still need to clarify the meaning of Keser on its highest level, even beyond the correlations of Ayin and the white fire, both of which have opposites: Yesh and black fire. Ultimately, Keser is the reality which maintains and roots all opposites, the essence that contains the white fire and the black fire, the Ayin and the Yesh, the spiritual and the physical, sleep and awakeness, Heaven and earth, along with every other opposite.

Generally, *Katnus* / smallness or immaturity, is a manifestation which precedes an opening into *Gadlus* / greatness, bigness, maturity. And in that scheme, the smaller the Katnus, the greater the Gadlus that follows it. For example, the development of an animal is very different than the development of a human being. Within an hour after birth, many animals are fully developed. "A day old ox is called an ox" (*Baba Kama*, 65b).

Sofer also contradicted this ruling and argued that since Yom Tov Sheini of Shavuos was never a Safek Yom Tov, it is a *Vadai* / certainty (of Chazal), and is thus more *Chamur* / stringent than the Safek of the second day of all other Yomim Tovim (Shu't *Chasam Sofer*, Orach Chayim, 145. See also, Shu't *Sho'el U-Meshiv*, vol. 1:150. And Vol. 2:85).

There is not much difference between a baby elephant and an adult elephant, other than size. A baby elephant is a complete elephant, just smaller and with less physical strength than an adult. A lizard, when it hatches, is already independent and ready to seek its prey, without any need for parental nurturance. A human being is the slowest developing 'animal.' It takes years before a child learns to walk and talk, let alone fend for itself. The Katnus of a human being is much 'smaller' than other life forms, but the Gadlus of the human being is correspondingly higher. After much development, a human being can choose to perform intellectually complex tasks beyond or even against his instinctual patterning.

From this perspective, Klal Yisrael went to sleep on the night before Matan Torah — they went into a state of Katnus — with the intention of opening up to a higher Gadlus. They crouched down so they could jump higher, as it were.

Similarly, when Hashem wanted to create Adam and Chavah as two separate beings who would be able to have a *Panim-el-Panim* / face-to-face relationship, Hashem put Adam into a slumber, induced in him a Katnus, a sleep state. Coming out of this contraction, Adam would be able to experience a higher form of Gadlus.

Klal Yisrael went to sleep on the night of Matan Torah because they wanted to wake up to a *Panim-El-Panim* encounter with Hashem.

From a different perspective, perhaps Klal Yisrael thought that the only way to experience Gadlus was within sleep itself, in a deep dream-state. Such a pure and transcendent encounter, they reasoned, could only be possible if their egoic selves were asleep and

unconscious. Thus, they chose to sleep as a form of *Bitul* / self-transcendence and immersion in the level of Ayin.

Yet, the truth is that A) we have already experienced a measure of Katnus during the seven week period of the Sefira, which
is compared to the seven days of 'separation' of spouses following
menstruation. B) More significantly, the level of Gadlus that we are
privy to on Shavuos is the Gadlus of Keser, the place of unification
of opposites. On Shavuos, being awake and being asleep, *Yesh* /
existence and *Ayin* / nothingness, are all the same.

Normal growth demands a deconstruction or 'Katnus' of the old
status, before a higher construction or 'Gadlus' can emerge. Just as
one crouches to jump, the lower the Katnus which we achieve, that
much higher is the Gadlus that we can reach. The old structure
needs to be nullified in Katnus, to be put to sleep, rendered as Ayin,
for the higher Yesh to emerge. Yet this paradigm is only true in a
world of hierarchies, of 'lower and higher.' But in the world of *Achdus* / true unity, there is a *Yichud* / oneness between the lower Yesh
and the *Yesh ha'Amiti* / True Existence.

Keser is the level of Anochi, a paradoxical inclusion of both Ayin
and Yesh. The word *Anochi* has the letters of *k'Ani* / like an Ani, like
Yesh, but these letters also spell *k'Ayin* / like nothingness, as Keser
embraces and transcends all of reality.

Keser is like a crown above the body that encompasses and tol-
erates all the opposites of the body, as it were. It equally crowns the
right side and the left, the lower body and the upper body. Similarly, it is the place where all is one with Hashem. *Yesh haNivrah*
/ created existence and *Yesh ha'Amiti* / the 'essence' of Hashem,

K'viyachol / as it were, are unified, as there is nothing else, Ein Od miL'vado, literally.

Yesh in numerical value is 310, and so twice *Yesh* (620) equals the numerical value of the word Keser. At Matan Torah we received the *Eser Dibros* / ten utterances, in which there are a total of 620 letters. This is the Keser of Torah. (These 620 also correspond to the 613 Mitzvos and 7 Mitzvos of the Sages = 620.) On Shavuos we receive the Gadlus of the Keser of Torah.

Since Keser is the paradoxical unification of both Ayin and Yesh, Gadlus and Katnus, it does not need to be preceded by a preparatory stage of Katnus. Keser is not a level that we can reach through a technique such as descending into a dream world or altered state. There is no need to experience Matan Torah during sleep, nor even in a special ego-less mode of consciousness. Keser is *Etzem* / Essence (in comparison to all that is revealed following Keser), and Essence embraces all expressions, all *Giluyim* / expressions, revelations — even including ego and normative waking consciousness.

In Keser there is a level that is called *Gal-Galta* / the skull. The word *Gal-Galta* is made up of the word *Gal* / wave, a movement upwards, twice. *Gal* is also the root of the word *Geulah*, a movement towards redemption, an upward movement towards our homeland, and inwardly, a rising towards one's authentic self. Yet, *Galus* / exile also contains the letters of *Gal*, as Galus is also a movement, but a movement away from our homeland, a sending away, and inwardly, a separation from our most authentic selves. As a dimension of Keser, *Gal-Galta* contains both of these: Geulah and Galus, Katnus and Gadlus, oneness and two-ness.

Experientially, when there is a revealing of this third level of Gadlus, everything 'makes sense'; even seemingly clashing opposites. We come to understand that everything, even our sense of *Chesaron* / lack and our 'failings' are one with our fullness and successes. They are part of our reason for being, our Keser. If you seem to lack talent in a certain area of your work, precisely because of that you might work harder and become more successful than if it had come easy to you. Then you will understand how everything in life, even your so-called failings, are actually your strengths, your crown of victory, who you are.

This Gadlus is a type of open-minded clarity in which life makes sense. It is second level Gadlus, Gadlus of Mochin of *Aba* (Chochmah), or first level Gadlus, Mochin of *Imah* (Binah). Then there is even a higher level, Gadlus Shelishi (Keser), in which all is clearly understood as perfect. Your mistakes are known to be completely good; the reason and purpose for everything that has happened in your life is openly revealed.

JOY IN THE YESH OF THE BODY, WHICH IS LINKED TO THE *Yesh* / ESSENCE OF THE CREATOR

As Shavuos is deeply associated with the *Etzem* / Essence of Hashem, this construct will help us decipher a certain seeming anomaly. On the one hand, all opinions agree that we must have a festive meal on Shavuos. Celebrating Shavuos, the illustrious Talmudic sage, Rav Yoseph would cook a special third-born calf, as the third born is considered the tastiest (*Pesachim*, 68b). In general, Matan Torah is connected to the 'third' as we learn, "Blessed be the Merciful One who gave a three-fold Torah (Torah, the Prophets and the Writings) to a three-fold people (Kohen, Levi and Yis-rael), through a third[-born] (Moshe was the third child of his family) on the third day (after couples had separated for 2 days at Mount Sinai) in the third month (of the year, Nisan being the first month)…" (*Shabbos,* 88a).

'Third' is also an allusion to the third level of Gadlus that we receive on Shavuos, and Rav Yoseph is teaching us that this Gad-lus of Keser is so utterly transcendent and all-embracing that it is reflected even in the foods we eat on Shavuos. Gadlus permeates all existence, even the density of our Yesh, to the extent that even in a 'mundane' state we can feel its expansiveness, openness and harmony with the Infinite One, the Creator of the physical and the spiritual (As will be explored in greater detail further on).

On Shavuos a festive meal is integral to the day. Even eating is an embodiment of receiving the Torah; the realm of Keser is felt in the physical body. Yet there is a contrast between the modes of embodiment on Shavuos and on Simchas Torah. On Simchas To-rah when the reading of the Torah cycle is completed, we celebrate with festive dancing, perhaps even on the streets. It is an outward expression of joy. When the Torah is given on Shavuos, our joy is more internal and subtle and there is no special manifestation of dancing and singing. It is a more subtle, cerebral experience, almost too internal to be manifest in intense emotion or expressive physi-cal movements. Why then is the physical act of eating highlighted but not dancing?

Shavuos is an experience of the *Etzem* / Essence of Hashem — as much as it is humanly possible to experience. Everything and every idea in this world, and beyond this world, has two properties, as it were: its Etzem and its *Giluyim* / expressions.

Dancing and openly expressed joy is a mode of Giluyim. The inner feelings of joy are actively communicated and demonstrated to the visible physical world. This activity implies a distinction between the inner and outer dimensions of experience. Extended dancing and singing can 'transport' us to a higher state of elation; there is a change in consciousness toward self-transcendence. An elated dancer might try to pull a serious or reticent looking person into the dance circle, implying that they need to actively change their state of emotion or transcend their self-consciousness. Dancing is a 'doing' more than a 'being.'

Of course Etzem-consciousness can embrace and include Giluyim; it does not suppress outward signs of joy, nor enforce a quiet physical appearance. Rather, the 'non-doing' of Etzem has no 'need' to outwardly express or suppress feelings, because there is no division or distance between inner feelings and an outer world. There is no urge to transform one's state and arouse feelings of elation because there is no real division between higher and lower states of consciousness. There is no separation between Heaven and earth. There is no preference for one emotional experience over another; there is no imposition of something extra to life as it is.

Since Shavuos is a celebration of Etzem, we function as Etzem — as our natural state of joyful being. Eating is 'essential'; it's not extra to life or a form of trance. Eating a delicious dinner with family or friends is not a way to spiritually ascend to a higher level, nor to nullify Yesh and enter Ayin. The Yesh of natural physical activity is already one with the Yesh haAmiti. Eating is a setting for the experience of a simple, internal, essential joy that does not necessarily call forth outward expressions such as dancing.

On Shavuos you are given the realization that there is nothing you must do; you already *are* your essence.

Essay Five
༜
THE FIFTIETH LEVEL:
Beyond the Possibility of Ra / Negativity & Sin

THERE ARE MANY TEACHINGS ABOUT SHAVUOS THAT SPEAK of Matan Torah, the value of Torah, and the effects of the revelation of Torah upon the world and human beings. But there is one teaching in the *Yerushalmi* / Jerusalem Talmud that is quite puzzling since it speaks of Shavuos as a day of radical atonement, not something that necessarily comes to mind when one thinks about Shavuos.

Here is what the Yerushalmi (*Rosh Hashanah*, 4:8) says, "With regards to all the offerings (in the Temple) the Torah uses the word *Cheit* / sin offering, but this is not so with the offering on Shavuos; here the Torah refers to the offering as *Se'ir Izim* / goats. Why? Hashem says to Klal Yisrael, 'Since you accepted the yoke of Torah, I will consider it as if you have *never* sinned.'"

The *Bavli* / Babylonian Talmud teaches that the negative in-fluence of the snake, the root of all sin, was eliminated when Klal Yisrael received the Torah (*Shabbos*, 156a). Had Klal Yisrael remained in the posture of 'receiving the Torah' they would have never again sinned. However, this teaching says nothing of their past, only their present and theoretical future. The Yerushalmi's statement is unique, "Since you accepted the yoke of Torah, I will consider it as if you had *never* sinned." This is a retroactive statement; every-thing of the past is erased and transformed. On an inner level, this means that at Matan Torah, Klal Yisrael attained a deep measure of Teshuvah. A level of such absolute conviction and commitment to the path of Torah that there's no possibility to even speak about negativity and sin, even what had already been done in the past.

ENDING THE YEAR & ITS CURSES, BEGINNING A NEW YEAR WITH ITS BLESSINGS

Twice the Torah speaks of the *Tochechah* / rebuke, the 'curses' that result when we break the covenant which we entered with Hashem. These consequences are outlined at the end of the Book of Vayikra and again towards the end of Devarim. We read the latter right before Rosh Hashanah, and we read the former right before Shavuos. In the words of our Sages (*Megilah*, 31b), "Ezra (the Scribe) instituted that we read from the Torah the curses in Vayikra before Shavuos, and the curses in Devarim before Rosh Hashanah; what is the reason? כדי שתכלה השנה וקללותיה / "so that *the year may end along with its curses*." In other words, we read the 'curses' at the end of the year, in order that any curses or unresolved issues should be resolved, so that we may begin anew.

Our Sages continue: "Granted, with regard to the curses in Devarim it is so you can say, 'so that the year should end along with its curses.' But as regards those in Vayikra — is Shavuos a New Year? ...Yes! Shavuos is also a New Year, as we have learned, 'Shavuos is the New Year for (the fruit of) the tree.'" Shavuos is an ending of the curses and misalignments of the past, and an opportunity to begin again, with a clean slate.

As previously discussed at length, Matan Torah followed 49 days of counting the Omer. However, the year that Klal Yisrael left Egypt they did not bring the Omer offering; they only brought it once they settled in the Land of Israel. What, therefore, does it mean that they counted 49 days of the Omer from the day after Pesach? *The Zohar* (3, 96b) teaches that Klal Yisrael 'counted' even though they did not bring the actual Omer. This is also what the *Ohr haChayim* (Emor, 23:15) writes (See also *Menachem Tziyon* (Riminov), Shemini). In any case, insofar as their focus in counting was not on the actual Omer, it represented what comes after 49, the concept of 50.

The number 50 is connected with the generation that left Egypt and with Moshe. There are 50 gates of understanding (*Rosh Hashanah*, 21b. *Nedarim*, 38a). In his lifetime Moshe attained only the 49th level of understanding (*ibid*), and thus he was unable to cross the Jordan River (whose width was 50 cubits (*Tosafos, Sotah* 34b)), and enter the Holy Land (See also Devarim, 3:25, *Ba'al haTurim*). Only at the moment of his death, when he had ascended Mount Nevo, did he attain the 50th level. The words *Mount Nevo*, which can be read as *the Mount Nun-Bo* / the Mount which has *Nun* (50), the 50th gate, *Bo* / in it.

BEYOND THE 49

There are 49 curses in the Book of Vayikra. In the Book of Devarim there are double that number, 98, which is fitting as Devarim is called the 'Repetition of the Torah' (See *Tosefos, Gittin,* 2a). The 49 days of the Omer cleanse us of the 49 curses of our active misalignment and *Katnus* / smallness or constriction.

Then comes the 50th day, the Gadlus and the giving of the Torah, when we receive a state beyond all negativity. When the Gadlus of Shavuos comes, there is a ceasing of all 'curses' and it is a completely new beginning; with the eradication of even the possibility of Katnus or violation of our Divine covenant.

Shavuos is thus not only the new year for the fruit of the tree, but also a new year for you. Our fruits, the results of our past actions, are re-set. The record of our past negativity and smallness is no more. We are allowed to enter into our maturity, aligned and unified with our own Gadlus, our limitless potential.

COMPLETE FREEDOM

The number 50 represents the *Yovel* / Jubilee, which is the concept of *Cheirus Olam* / eternal freedom.

The Torah asks us to count seven weeks, but it also asks us to count 50 days. These 50 days are a hint to the idea of Yovel, when land reverted to its original owner and slaves went free. The Beis Ya'akov (Part 3: Parshas Behar) explains that Yovel is a time when everything and everyone returns to its source. When you truly live from your Source, you do not need an intermediary. A slave 'needs' his master to connect to who he is. But when Yovel comes along he no longer needs his master, as he returns to the 'master' within himself, he is free.

At Mount Sinai, on the 50th day, a day of complete freedom, a time when we received the Torah (which is the deepest freedom), we no longer needed an intermediary or anyone to help us connect with Hashem. We all heard *Anochi Hashem Elokechah* / "I Am Hashem *your* (in the singular) G-d," meaning that Hashem was revealed to each person on their own level. Each heard 'I belong to you! I am your own most intimate Source.'

Shemitah is the seventh year of an agricultural cycle in which fields and trees in Eretz Yisrael are allowed to rest. Whereas Yovel provides full freedom for slaves, people, in Shemitah there is a freedom for fields, for the earth itself. Shemitah is symbolized by the last letter in the Four Letter Name of Hashem (Yud-Hei-Vav and Hei), also called the 'lower' Hei. Yovel corresponds to the second letter of the Name, the 'upper' Hei (*Zohar* 3, 108a).

The last three letters of the Name, Hei, Vav, Hei together spell *Hoveh* / 'is' or present being. So when the Vav (the six active *Sefiros* / emotional attributes) connects with the lower Hei (Malchus, the receptive attribute below) there are a total of seven one-dimensional Sefiros. However, when the upper Hei (Binah, fullness of understanding) connects with the Vav-Hei below, the 'seven' multiply and a fullness of dimensionality manifests as seven-times-seven, the 49 gates of Binah. The 'understanding' represented by the upper Hei is experienced as freedom, for your emotional attributes are balanced by their higher intellect. Furthermore, the Sefiros below are now inter-included, and this is why they are no longer one-dimensional; each one 'understands' and is balanced by the others. Since Chesed, for example, includes Gevurah, Tiferes, and the rest of the seven Sefiros. Each of the seven includes seven dimensions, there are now 49 Sefiros.

Reactive emotion is 'one-dimensional' and is not 'free.' Without Binah, if someone triggers one of your inner imbalances you will get upset or flare up in anger. Pro-active emotions, by contrast, are measured. And, as they are permeated by the influence of Binah, each emotion contains traces of the others. Since you are coming from a place of higher intellect, you can stand back and blend your response appropriately for the situation. For instance, if an emotion of Gevurah or withholding is stimulated in you, you will be aware of it and you can choose to blend your response with the compassion of Tiferes.

The students of Rebbe Akiva died because they did not respect each other. Surely they 'loved' each other, as they were dedicated to the guidance of their teacher who said, "To love your friend as yourself, this is the great principle of Torah." However, their love, their Chesed, was one dimensional — it was only love, without the boundaries and counter-balances brought by higher awareness. The Tikun for this syndrome is to detach and balance ourselves, to 'blend' our Sefiros. An opportune time to grow in this ability is the period of Sefiras haOmer, during which time Rebbe Akiva's students died. The product of this inner work is higher and higher levels of freedom, until the 49th level is reached and the state of Yovel can descend upon us.

Freedom from reactivity is actually a lower form of freedom. Resting from all reactions and remaining silent when emotions are stimulated can also be one-dimensional, as you are 'only' silent. This lower freedom corresponds to *Shemitah* / resting the land. Shemitah only requires that we 'cease working.' This is the lower Hei, whose interaction with emotions can only contain one of each Sefirah at once. In such a case, when you are inspired to withhold 'taking' from another, you might be able to only express 'giving,' even when it may be to the detriment of the other. Then, if a person asked you for a cup of water to drink, you might end up giving him the hose.

Both Shemitah and Yovel represent rest, and the letter Hei is a 'restful' or silent letter. When Hei comes at the end of a word it is not pronounced; it is merely a restful release of breath, a ceasing from the 'work' of enunciating consonants, as it were.

Malchus or 'earth' is represented by the lower Hei. The elevation of the lower Hei thus involves ceasing from working and manipulating the land. However, complete human freedom is not only freedom in the realm of actions, but freedom in the realm of thinking and awareness. That higher freedom comes from Binah, the higher Hei. The deepest level of Binah, with its inter-including effects, is freedom from all constricted consciousness.

Pesach / Passover is a physical freedom, freedom from enslaved work. However, we are not completely free until Shavuos, the liberation and opening of awareness corresponding to the higher Hei. Complete freedom can only be revealed by the ways of Binah. At Matan Torah we receive a freedom in the zone of destiny and purpose.

We received the physical *Luchos* / tablets in the continuation of the Matan Torah event. In the Luchos, the Divine Utterances were *Charus* / engraved within stone. *Charus* is related to the word *Cheirus* / freedom. When we receive the Torah we become completely *free* both physically and mentally. We are no longer enslaved to our *Yetzer haRa* / inclination toward negativity (*Zohar* 3, 97b), in consciousness, thought, word and deed. We even become free from the Angel of Death (*Medrash Rabbah*, Shemos, 41). This is the level of 50, total and eternal release from all *Katnus* / smallness and ego; freedom from sin and reactivity.

THE 50TH LEVEL

Fifty is absolute *Tov* / goodness, *Gadlus* / expansiveness, openness, positivity, eternity, transcendence, with no alternative or even possibility of the opposite. Forty-nine is the place of our choice, our Bechirah, where we have the choice to choose life or death, blessings or curses, light or darkness.

"Had the Torah been given in a clear cut form one would have no ground to stand on. 'Moshe said to Hashem, 'Master of the Universe, tell me how the law (of the Torah) should be decided.' Hashem said to him, 'Follow the majority." If the majority declares the accused exempt, declare him exempt. If the majority declares him liable, declare him liable. This is so the Torah may be expounded in 49 ways that something is impure and 49 ways that something is pure" (Yerushalmi, *Sanhedrin*, 4:2. *Medrash Rabbah*, Vayikra, 26:2. *Medrash Tehilim*, 12:4. In Bavli, *Eiruvin*, 13b, we find the phrase, "48 reasons to purify and 48 reasons to impurify").

'Seven' corresponds to our world, as in the seven days of Creation. This is the world of duality, the world of 'good and evil,' and the realm of free-choice. In the world of 49 there is a possibility for purity and also the possibility for impurity. The fullness of seven is 49.

Even when one makes a choice to live a life of purity, of Torah and Mitzvos, there is always the possibility of slipping, falling, and reverting to the opposite. Such is the nature of the world of free choice. The opposite of good lurks below each good choice and every good thing. This can work to our advantage however. A person who chose to live a life of impurity, negativity and Katnus, also has the possibility to reset his life through Teshuvah; radical positive change is always available.

On the 50th level of *Kedushah* / holiness and purity, which is *Tov b'Etzem* / essentially good, there is no possibility for the opposite choice. This is a place beyond the *Nekudah* / point of *Bechirah* / free choice. On this level, when one chooses a life of purity, Torah and Mitzvos, holiness and connection, Gadlus and Deveikus, that choice is so dramatic and pervasive that it leaves the person with no alternative or option to choose anything else.

כל פעל ה למענהו וגם־רשע ליום רע / Hashem made *Kol* ("everything") for His praise — *v'Gam* ("and even") the wicked man for the day of evil (Mishlei, 16:4). *Kol* in numerical value is 50. In the world of Kol, everything that is created is for Hashem's praise, there is only goodness, it is a place beyond Bechirah, where there is no possibility for *Ra* / negativity, and everything is for Hashem's praise. This is the deeper meaning of the first part of this verse.

Then the verse continues, *v'Gam Rasha* / "and even the wicked man..." *V'Gam* is numerically 49; in the world of 49, there is still the possibility for a *Rasha* or a 'day of evil.'

THE SYMBOL OF 50

Before returning to the discussion of reaching the 50th level, let us explore a couple more symbolic meanings of the number 50 in TaNaCh and its relationship to the world of absolute goodness and holiness.

The going out of Egypt is mentioned in the Torah 50 times (*Zohar* 2, 85b. 3, 262a. *Tikunei Zohar*, Tikun 32). These correspond to the 50 days of Sefirah, i.e., the 49 that we count, plus one for the day of Shavuos. In general, there are 50 'gates' of Binah; 49 levels of understanding that we can climb, and a 50th level that can only be granted as a gift from Above (*Rosh Hashanah*, 21b. *Nedarim*, 38a). At Matan Torah we were gifted and received the 50th level.

Matan Torah is like our wedding day (*Shir haShirim*, 3:11. Rashi, "The day of the giving of the Torah, when they crowned Him King for themselves and accepted His yoke." See also the end of *Ta'anis*, regarding the day they received the Second Luchos). In marriage, the amount of the Kesuvah, in a normal situation, is 200 Zuz or Dinars, which equal 50 silver Shekels (the amount needed to pay by a man who, *Chas veShalom*, violates or seduces a woman (*Devarim*, 22:29. *Kesuvos*, 10a)).

Rabbeinu Bachya (*Bereishis*, 4:3) brings down from the Medrash that the story of Kayin and Hevel happened on the 50th day of Creation (or their creation). The Medrash says that Kayin and Hevel lived for 50 days (*Medrash Rabbah*, Bereishis, 22:4). Hevel was killed on his 50th day and so we bring an offering on the 50th day after being 'born.' This corresponds to how, as a people, we left Egypt and on the 50th day we received the Torah (*Rabbeinu Bachya*, Bereishis, 4:3). Matan Torah is a Tikun for this first death in history.

Our offering on Shavuos was vegetative, similar to the offering from Kayin, and this perhaps helped with his Tikun. With Matan Torah we moved from the Hevel mode of life, nomadic shepherding, to the Kayin mode; and this culminated when we eventually settled in the Holy Land and began working the land. This too hints at the rectification of the soul of Kayin.

The Medrash notes that an apple takes 50 days to ripen and that this occurs in the month of Sivan (*Shir haShirim Rabbah* 2:2). This is a reference to the 50-day period between Pesach and Shavuos, during which the Jewish nation 'ripened' and developed until they could embrace the Torah. The 'apple' is a symbol of the declaration, *Na'aseh v'Nishmah* / "We will do and we will hear," which we declared at Sinai (*Shabbos*, 88a. See Tosafos, ad loc., for how the 'apple' refers to the Esrog).

There were 50 golden hooks upon the roof of the Mishkan, spread directly above the curtain cover at the entrance of the *Kodesh haKedoshim* (Shemos 26:6. See *Rokeach*, Shemos 26:6, p.141, for how the 50 golden hooks attaching the curtains parallel the 50 times the word *Torah* is mentioned in the singular in Chumash). The Mishkan was a 'portable Mount Sinai' where the 50th level of consciousness was revealed, and where we could interact with Hashem's Presence directly.

Upon the garments of the *Kohen Gadol* / High Priest — the most essential figure in the Mishkan — were affixed the names of the 12 *Shevatim* / Tribes of Israel. These names were written on two stones affixed to the shoulders of his *Ephod* / Apron. There were six names consisting of 25 letters on each of the two stones, totalling 50 letters (*Sotah* 36a-b). The Baal haTurim writes (on Bamidbar, 10:35), that Moshe wanted to take the Shevatim, who have 50 letters, over the Jordan River, which was 50 Amos wide (*Sifri*, VaEschanan, 29). Centuries later, and towards the end of the time period of the Mishkan, King David received 50 shekels from each Shevet to purchase the mountain in Jerusalem which would become the place of the Beis haMikdash. Alternatively, David purchased the site of the altar for 50 Shekalim (*Zevachim*, 116b. See also *Sukkah*, 53a and *Sifri*, Nasso 42).*

All the above deepens the correspondence of '50' with absolute Tov, atonement, holiness and unification with Hashem.

A MOUNTAIN OVER THEIR HEADS

At Matan Torah the 50th level, the level of 'we had never sinned,' was revealed. We reached a point beyond Bechirah, duality, ego and eventual death. We entered a world of eternal purity, goodness and Kedushah. This is the deeper meaning of Hashem 'suspending the mountain over their heads.'

---

* One verse says, "David gave to Ornan for the place 600 shekels of gold by weight" (*Divrei haYamim* 1, 21:25). Whereas it is also written, "So David bought the threshing-floor and the oxen for 50 shekels of silver" (*Shemuel* 2, 24:24). How can these be reconciled? He collected 50 [shekels] from each tribe, which amounted to 600 [in all]. Rebbe said... [He bought] the oxen, wood, and site of the altar for fifty, and [the site of] the whole Beis haMikdash for six hundred.

Our Sages tell us (*Shabbos*, 88a), "'And they stood *under* the Mount'...This teaches (since it says 'under' the Mount as opposed to 'near the Mount') that the Holy One, blessed be He, overturned the mountain upon them like an inverted barrel, and said to them, 'If you accept the Torah, good, if not, this shall be your burial.'" The obvious question is that Klal Yisrael had already said *Na'aseh v'Nishmah* / we will do and we will hear (as *Tosefos* asks); they already willfully accepted upon themselves to follow the ways of the Torah, so why the seeming coercion?

One way of looking at the suspended mountain is that it represents an absolute resolve to accept the yoke of Torah (*Torah Ohr*, Megilas Esther, 98d). Their commitment to Torah was so absolute and unequivocal that it was 'as if' a mountain was suspended over their heads. They felt there was no alternative for them; it was 'Torah or death.' Someone looking in from the outside would think that a mountain had been threateningly suspended over their heads, when in fact, this deepest of commitments came from within, from the force of their own desire for Torah, their own *Na'aseh v'Nishmah*.

Their *Na'aseh v'Nishmah* was such that their acceptance of Torah was no longer a choice, rather, an expression of who they were and their very lifeforce. In life, we may have a freedom to choose, but we do not have a freedom to choose or not choose — choosing is synonymous with life. Some people seemingly 'choose not to choose' and live their lives on autopilot, yet even in that case a choice was rendered. Torah is life itself. Once they said *Na'aseh v'Nishmah* they realized that Torah was their very life and something beyond choice; they were *happily* compelled. This is the 50th level, absolute purity, goodness and Kedushah.

The mountain over their heads was a manifestation of their own desire to accept Torah beyond choice, 'This desire compels us so completely, it is as if a mountain were suspended over us.' (Conversely, Hashem's choice in us is not because of any 'reason,' whether for our righteousness or our good deeds; rather it was a *Bechirah Klalis* / general choice. For this reason, "when Klal Yisrael came to receive the Torah, Hashem suspended the mountain over their heads, that they would be forced to accept the Torah"; thus accepting the Torah beyond 'reason' (Maharal, *Netzach Yisrael*, p. 71).) They chose to catapult themselves to a place of such connection to Hashem that there was no longer any *Bechirah* / choice; their only option was to receive goodness, life, blessings, Torah and Mitzvos.

In the world of 49, duality and free choice, good and evil, are all אפשרי המציאות / *Efshari haMetziyus* / possibilities of existence — there is a possibility to choose goodness and there is a possibility to choose the opposite. This is the world of the 'Tree of Knowledge; Good and Evil.' On the 50th level, however, *Tov* / goodness is a מחוייב המציאות / *Mechuyav haMetziyus* / absolute given, an unconditional or 'necessary' existence.

Goodness on the level of Mechuyav haMetziyus precludes a *Yetzer haRa* / inclination or attraction to negativity. The feeling is that there is no longer any possibility to choose or even relate to *Ra* / evil. To live is to manifest goodness and holiness. If one would not engage in Torah and Mitzvos, then one would consider himself 'buried.'

This experience of acceptance of the revelation repeats itself every year at the same time. We choose to receive Torah in such a manner that all our negativity, and even the possibility of negativity and sin, is erased. There is a ceasing of all the '49 curses' and a radical new beginning. The scars of the past are gone. We are free from all negativity, ego, resentment, constriction and *Katnus* / smallness. Our mistakes have become merits. There is only absolute goodness.

Essay Six
ᘎ
MATAN TORAH:
The Day the Torah was Given
Receiving the Torah Every Day Anew

O N SHABBOS WE REST IN REMEMBRANCE OF THE CULMI-
NATION of the days of Creation. "In six days Hashem created the world and rested on the seventh." On the 15th
of Nisan we celebrate our going out of Egypt, and the word *Pesach*
means *passed over*, as Hashem passed over the homes of Klal Yisrael and spared them from the final plague. The revelation and giving
of the Torah on Mount Sinai is perhaps the most important event
in our history, yet surprisingly the Torah does not clearly specify its
date. *Shavuos* simply means 'weeks' as it follows the counting of the
49 days of the Omer, which are seven weeks. Why is the historically unprecedented event of Matan Torah not clearly delineated
or dated in the Torah? Through analysis, we can determine that it

was either on the sixth or seventh of Sivan, but the Torah itself is mysteriously ambiguous.

In the *Nusach* / liturgy of prayer we call Shavuos *Z'man Matan Toraseinu* / the time of the giving of our Torah. We do not say *Z'man Bikurim* / the time of first fruit offerings in the Beis ha-Mikdash, although the Torah does give Shavuos this name. This is because in prayer we specifically thank Hashem for the blessings and goodness bestowed upon us. (Similarly, the Nusach does not refer to Pesach as *Z'man Korban Pesach* / the time of the Passover offering, or *Z'man Achilas Maror* / the time of eating bitter herbs, rather it calls Pesach *Z'man Cheiruseinu* / the time of our freedom.) Yet, the question still remains: why does the Torah not call Shavuos simply *Shavuos* instead of *Z'man Matan Toraseinu?*

There is also something peculiar with regards to the place, the space where Matan Torah occurred. It did not happen in a civilized area, rather in a *Midbar* / desert, wilderness, a no-man's land. Say our Sages (*Medrash Rabba*, Bamidbar, 1:7), "Just as a wilderness is free to all the inhabitants of the world, so too are the words of Torah free to them." The Midbar is a place of *Hefker* / ownerless property, and anyone can freely travel therein; the same is true with Torah, it is free to all who seek it. *Hefker* can mean two things: the object does not belong to anyone, or, since no one in particular owns it, everybody owns it. No particular person, not even Moshe, owns the Torah. It is an inheritance to us all.

Furthermore, the Torah was not given in a place that was populated by a certain people or within a certain culture or historical context. If the Torah had been given in Ancient Egypt, for example, or for that matter in a Shtetel in Eastern Europe, the Jews in America or elsewhere might say that the Torah is no longer applicable or even relevant to them.

The Torah does not belong to a specific culture or historical period, nor to a specific place and time. Why? This communicates the fact that the Torah is timeless and spaceless.

'THE GIVING' VS. 'THE RECEIVING' OF TORAH

The spaceless, timeless and ownerless character of Matan Torah is particularly important from the perspective of the recipient; for something to be given, the recipient must receive it. Since the receiving of Torah is not exclusively tied to a certain Yom Tov or Shul or *Beis Medrash*, it may be received anew every day, in every place, and by any person who is sincerely receptive.

While Matan Torah occurred on Shavuos and is intrinsically related to that day, *Kabalas haTorah* / the receiving of the Torah permeates all space, time and consciousness.

"The words of the Torah shall be new to you as if they were just given today" (Rashi, from *Tanchuma*, Shemos 19:1). This implies that Hashem gives us the Torah continuously; Hashem is the *Nosen haTorah* / One giving (present tense) the Torah. The sound of the Voice at Mount Sinai never ceased. This is certainly true from the cosmic perspective; and from our perspective we need to receive the Torah anew every moment.

"Every day, let the Torah be *as dear to you* as if you had received it this day at Mount Sinai" (Rashi, *Tanchumah*, Devarim, 26:16). The Torah is 'new' each day, and thus every day brings a new experience of To-rah and a renewal that awakens an excitement to grow and discover more and more wisdom.

In the times of the Beis haMikdash there was a Mitzvah to of-fer *Bikurim* / new fruits on Shavuos day. The newness of the first produce of the year created a physical association with the newness of the Torah which we were accepting upon ourselves. Each year when the farmer picked his new fruits he experienced a sense of renewal. However when he brought them to the Mikdash as Bi-kurim, a *Bas Kol* / Heavenly voice rang forth, "You have brought the first fruits today — you shall be privileged to do so next year too" (*Rashi*, Devarim, 26:16). In other words, his excitement and re-newal brought forth a fervor to continue. It is the same with us when we receive Torah upon ourselves anew.

MAKING OURSELVES AS *Hefker* / OWNERLESS AND HUMBLY TRANSPARENT

Why was the Torah given in a desert? Another reason given in the previously quoted Medrash is so we will understand that, "Anyone who does not make *himself* Hefker like the desert, cannot acquire the Torah." / כל מי שאינו עושה עצמו כמדבר, הפקר, אינו יכול לקנות את החכמה והתורה

On one level, the Medrash is telling us about the positive quality of *Bitul* / selfless humility. Indeed, to be open to receive the Torah we need humility, much like Moshe, the humblest of men (*Bamid-bar*, 12:3). In his absolute humility, Moshe became the conduit for the revelation of Torah to Klal Yisrael. It is for this same reason that the Torah was given on the otherwise 'unremarkable' Mount

Sinai — a mountain that was shorter than others. "Hashem disregarded all of the other mountains and hills, and rested His Divine Presence on the lowly Mount Sinai" (*Sotah*, 5a). Without humility a person cannot accept a higher authority or higher state of wisdom.

Besides the experience of humility, this Medrash is also telling us something about how to assimilate the wisdom of the Torah; how to prepare our minds to truly receive Torah. To receive the Torah anew every day, we need to continuously shed our sense of possessiveness and ownership of what we think we know. We need to let our minds become Hefker and open, like a no-man's land into which Hashem's Presence can descend.

A full cup cannot be filled. We need to let go of past experiences and open ourselves up to the Torah and its texts. We need to step out of the way and allow the Torah to reveal Herself. Every day and every moment something new and wonderful, surprising and magical will then unfold before us; for nothing in Torah is actually old, stale, or already known. Even if you learn the same teaching 100 times, the 101st time will be incomparable. Torah is one with the *Ein Sof* / Infinite One.

So stand in awe before the Infinitely colossal and majestic Torah. Simply and humbly open your mind and heart. Be surprised by the layers upon layers of its mystery. Of course we need to be *Misyagea* / toiling, engaging and stretching our minds to understand what we can of the Divine Intellect, especially as it filters through the Torah she-b'al-Peh given over to human understanding. But, simultaneously, we need to be still and open ourselves until the inner *Sod* / secret of Torah becomes revealed to us; day after day another layer peels away and the core of Truth shines more brightly.

We need to immerse again and again in the endless *Hischadshus* / newness of Torah, the vast sea of Talmud, and all the powerful and unceasing rivers of Divine wisdom constantly flowing from Gan Eden. Know that that 'water' flows to the lowest of places.

Essay Seven

CONNECTING TO THE WHITE & BLACK FIRES OF THE TORAH & THEIR UNITY

*A*T MATAN TORAH WE RECEIVED THE KESER OF Torah, the *Klal Gadol* / greatest of principles, namely, the Oneness of the Infinite Source of All. From the Klal Gadol flows all the *Pratim* / details of the Torah. The root of all the *Kavanos* / mindful intentions of the Arizal, that we should entertain during the Yom Tov of Shavuos and specifically on the night of Shavuos, is to be open to receive the level of Keser. Keser is also called the *Sherashei haMochin* / source of intelligence; another name for the deep truth that was revealed at Matan Torah.

Every Prat / detail of Torah wisdom is a *Klal* / generality in comparison with the many other Pratim that flow from it in turn. In relationship to the rest of the Torah, the *Eser Dibros* / Ten Commandments are the Keser, the Klal of the entire Torah — each of the 613 Mitzvos are rooted in one of the Ten Commandments, as Rav Saadia Gaon, the great Babylonian scholar (882-942 CE) delineates (As quoted by *Rashi*, "All 613 Mitzvos are included in the Ten Commandments..." (Shemos, 24:12)). There are 620 words in the Ten Commandments, which in turn correspond to the 613 Biblical Mitzvos and the 7 Rabbinic Mitzvos (*Baal Haturim*, Shemos, 20:14). The numerical value of the word *Keser* is 620 (*Shaloh*, Meseches Shavuos). Indeed, the first letter of the Ten Dibros is Aleph, from the word *Anochi*, and the last letter is Chaf. The sum of their numerical values (Chaf/20 plus Aleph/1) is 21, and this is the value of the Name *Ehe'yeh*, the Name revealed to Moshe at the burning bush. According to many opinions the Name *Ehe'yeh* is connected with the Divine attribute of Keser.

In terms of the Ten Commandments, the first two are the Keser, the Klal, of all the other eight. Our Sages tell us that this is because only the first two Commandments were directly transmitted to the people, whereas the subsequent eight Commandments had to be transmitted through Moshe (*Makos*, 24a. Rashi, Shemos, 19:19). *Anochi Hashem*, the First Commandment, is the root of all the other 248 positive directives, those that require us to do certain positive actions. The Second Commandment, 'you shall not have the gods of others,' is the root of all the 365 negative commandments, those that tell us to abstain from specific negative actions.

In terms of the first two commandments, the first, *Anochi Hashem*, is the Klal. From this perspective, *Anochi Hashem* is the *Klal Gadol baTorah* / great principle of Torah, and all of Torah is an unfolding of the implications of *Anochi Hashem*; all of Torah is rooted in *Anochi Hashem* (*Maor vaShemesh*, Yisro, in the name of Reb Elimelech).

One way to understand this is that if we truly believe in the revelation, 'I am Hashem, the Creator and Master of the Universe,' and there is nothing else than That, how then could we possibly not do the Mitzvos? Performing all the Mitzvos is a natural imperative and result of realizing *Anochi Hashem*. Indeed, from this perspective, *Anochi Hashem* was all that Klal Yisrael heard themselves at Mount Sinai.

In terms of the first *Dibur* / commandment, its first word, *Anochi*, is the Klal, the Keser of the entire Torah. Hashem's *I*, Hashem's Existence, so to speak, is thus the essence of the entire Torah. From this perspective what Klal Yisrael heard was just the word *Anochi*, and all the details and implications flowed from this simple principle.

The Mei haShiloach (also found in the Radziner) writes that when Klal Yisrael heard *Anochi Hashem* they also heard the phrase, "*Bereishis Bara* / In the beginning was created…" This means they heard the unity within Creation, Hashem is One with the world. There is no 'command' of 'You shall know that…' in *Anochi Hashem*; it is simply 'I Am!' When there is such an intense level of revealing, there is no separate Commander or commanded. Thus there is no need for a so-called command. And yet, all the Commandments flow from this 'white fire.'

In terms of the first word, *Anochi*, its first letter, Aleph, is the Keser, the Klal of the entire Torah. From this perspective, all that Klal Yisrael heard and needed to hear was *Ah*, the sound of the Aleph. Aleph is related to the word *Aluf* / chief, and thus it refers to the *Alufo Shel Olam* / Chief of the Universe, the Creator. Aleph means *one*; once Klal Yisrael assimilated the Aleph, the knowledge of the Oneness of the Creator, deeply into their consciousness, everything else was just commentary.

Whereas the word *Anochi* is *Dibur* / speech, a word, the Aleph is a *Kol* / sound. 'Sound' is deeper and simpler than speech. For speech to occur, there first needs to be a *Kol* / sound, a voice. For speech to occur there are a minimum of two stages. First, a unified and undifferentiated *Kol* / voice or 'sound' originating deep within, i.e., from the lungs. This is the level of the Kol prior to any articulation or specific meaning. The second stage of speech happens when this primordial sound passes through the throat and then to the tongue, palate, teeth and lips, in such a way that a distinct *Dibur* / utterance or 'word' is formed.

The *Ah* of the Aleph is called a *Kol Pashut* / simple wholesome sound (*Siddur Admur haZaken*, Kavanos haMikvah, p. 314). Indeed, every sound begins in the simple open 'space' of this *Ah*. As the Baal Shem Tov teaches, "There is no word, big or small, that does not contain an Aleph" (*Degel Machanei Ephrayim*, Likutim). Aleph is the root of the letters of Creation (Leshem, *Hakdamos v'Shearim*, Sha'ar haPone Kadim, 6). The Medrash teaches that the three letters spelling the word *Aleph* (Aleph, Lamed, Pei) make up an acronym for the phrase *Eftecha Lashon Peh* / I will open the language of your mouth (*Osyos d'Rebbe Akiva*, Aleph). In other words, the Aleph opens up the possibility for all language and sound. It is the source and beginning of speech, of Dibur; it is the Keser and the Klal of all speech.

And so, what Klal Yisrael heard at Mount Sinai, and what we can hear on Shavuos, is the *Kol Pashut*, the first revelation or sound-vibration of the Infinite Oneness entering the world of duality.

On an even deeper level, Reb Mendel, the Vorker Rebbe, once quipped that at Mount Sinai all that Klal Yisrael really heard was the mysterious innermost silence which preceded the sound of the Aleph of *Anochi*. Prior to Dibur is Kol, and prior Kol is the silence of Keser, the level called *Atik* / removed Transcendence. When Klal Yisrael reached the Sea of Reeds and many of them started praying to Hashem for help, Hashem told Moshe, "Why do you cry out to Me? Speak to the people of Israel and they shall journey forward" (*Shemos*, 14:15). The Zohar teaches on this verse that this event expresses, and is intrinsically connected to, the mystery of Atik. Atik corresponds to the *silence beyond sound*, the Ein Sof, the Infinite Oneness that is beyond sound or expression and can only be indicated by silence. This is the experience of Matan Torah, the experience of Shavuos.

The Keser of Torah is projected into the world of speech and duality, defined into words and sentences; each letter is distinct from the next and each word is separate from the other — the 'black fire' of Torah. However, at Mount Sinai, we experienced the 'white fire' of Torah, the Torah of Atzilus, the Torah of the Tree of Life, the Revelation of *Yichud* / non-separation, where All is One.

At Mount Sinai, teaches Rebbe Akiva (*Chagigah*, 6a; *Zevachim*, 115b), both the Klal *and* all the Pratim of the Torah were revealed. This means Klal Yisral grasped the ultimate silence of the Oneness of Hashem, but they also experienced how it unfolds and permeates all the Pratim of the Torah. They experienced the silence prior to the letter Aleph as it illumines the Aleph, which illumines the first word *Anochi*, which illumines the first two commandments, which shines as the eight commandments, which radiates as the entire Written Torah and all of the Oral Torah. They experienced the Torah as it illumines the entire world in all its multiplicity, as the world is but a *Roshem* / imprint of the Torah (*Shaloh*, Shavuos, Perek Torah Ohr, 34).

On Shavuos we receive the white fire Torah as it turns to flow back into the black fire Torah. We receive the Torah from its highest Source, within the Keser of the King, the place where there is שעשועי המלך בעצמותו / *Sha'ashu'ei haMelech b'Atzmuso* / the King taking Pleasure within Himself. We are shown how the Torah is *Nimshach* / drawn in a flow from the Infinite Source of Torah, which is the Source of all life, downwards into our defined four-dimensional universe; and into narratives, laws and activities which interact with every detail of our 'mundane' human experience.

At Mount Sinai, and on every Shavuos henceforth, there is a flow of revelation from the white fire back into the black fire. Throughout the rest of the year, as the Bnei Yissaschar teaches, to access the inner light or white fire of the Torah, we need to toil and ponder deeply the black fire of Torah. Through immersing in the black fire 'below,' we can get a glimpse of the white fire 'Above.' Through struggling with the black fire, expanding the possibilities and dimensions of reason and stretching the limits of logic, we can dip into an infinite expanse, the ever-flowering and flowing world of the white fire.

On Shavuos, however, this movement is reversed. Torah flows from Above to below, from white fire into black fire. Regarding Matan Torah it says, "And Hashem descended unto Mount Sinai." We did not physically or symbolically climb to the top of the mountain to receive the Torah; it descended to us. And so, in order for the lower realm to become a proper vessel to receive the Infinite Wisdom — the Keser of Keser, the White Fire that is One with the Ein Sof — the lower realm needed to 'cease' as a finite existence. That is, Klal Yisrael needs to be in a posture of 'silencing' their ego, so their finite selves can be open to receive Infinity.

We came to the mountain as individual people with separate egos, ambitions, dreams, manners of thinking and feeling, yet, we encamped at the mountain "as one person with one heart" (*Rashi*, Shemos, 19:2). This cessation of ego and separation was the most critical precondition for receiving the Torah. However, this was not only an intrapersonal silence, they also needed to experience a type of inner silencing and stillness, an absence of all internal 'black fire' and conventional self-perception, in order to be proper vessels to receive the white fire of the Torah.

Our Sages tell us (*Medrash Rabbah*, Shir haShirim, 1:12) that Klal Yisrael slept the entire night before Matan Torah, "because sleep on Atzeres (another name for Shavuos) is *Areivah* / sweetly pleasant" / לפי ששינה של עצרת ערבה. It was such a blissful sleep that on that night, says the Medrash, even the normally biting flies (called *Purtana*) were not perceived to be biting. On the morning of Matan Torah they were still experiencing such extremely pleasant deep sleep, that Hashem had to wake them up to give them the Torah.

This is a very perplexing Medrash. When they left Egypt they were told that the very objective of leaving Egypt would be to "serve Hashem on the Mountain," meaning to receive the Torah. From the day after they left Egypt they counted down the days until they would be ready to receive the Torah. For 49 days they counted each day to get closer to Matan Torah (The *Ran*, Pesachim, at the end in the name of the Medrash. *Sefer Hachinuch*, Mitzvah 306). Even though that year they did not bring the Omer (as the Omer offering was only to be brought once Klal Yisrael settled in the Land of Israel), they still counted down in order to purify themselves (*Zohar* 3, 96b) and prepare for Matan Torah. For 49 days, starting from the day after leaving Egypt, they counted with anticipation and yearning for this consummately meaningful moment — and then on the night before they slept peacefully, and even overslept. How could this have been possible?

Imagine, you get engaged and are so excited to get married that you are literally counting down the days until the Chupah. Or, you have planned the vacation of a lifetime and you are counting down the days until you depart. Imagine that your flight is booked for 50 days from now, at 6:00am. What would happen the night before the trip? Even if you were able to get some sleep, like many people, you might lie awake thinking about the wedding or the trip halfway or even all through the night or perhaps wake up periodically to check the time. Certainly most people would not enjoy an especially long or deep sleep. But Klal Yisrael slept in, as if it was just a long weekend, like a morning with no appointments and nothing to do.

This completely unexpected behavior compels us to say that their sleeping was somehow related to a strategy of receiving the Torah, not just to being well-rested for Matan Torah. In some way they intended to receive the Torah in their sleep (*Likkutei Sichos*, 4, p. 1024-1027). They went to sleep and stayed asleep, intentionally, so that at Matan Torah their bodies and egos would be nullified and they would receive the Torah in an egoless soul-level, as an out-of-body experience.

Another way of saying this is that they wanted to receive the Torah into their subconscious minds by means of being in the dream-state. During waking ours our minds are alive, thinking, and continually trying to make sense of the world. The left brain is active and alert, ensuring the survival of the ego and sense of self. When a person goes to sleep these guards come down; mental survival mechanisms are suspended and the more imaginative mind takes over. And that is what they wanted to utilize by going to sleep. They wanted to go beyond the intellectual mind, transcend the space of distinctions and dualities, and receive the Torah directly into the depths of their imaginative and subconscious minds.

They believed that inducing a dream state would be a more proper technique to receive the Transcendence of the Torah, rather than remaining in a seemingly 'mundane' waking state. True, the Divine logic of the Torah is a 'logic,' but it is also connected with the Ein Sof beyond all logic. Since they were going to receive the post-logical white fire, the simple sound of the Aleph of *Anochi*, the Keser of the Torah, they realized that they too needed to be 'infinite,' meaning no longer anchored in a conventional four-dimensional universe of strict logic. They wanted to experience the ineffability of the Infinite Creator's Presence within the Torah.

Their aspiration was to unify with the Source of the Torah, to experience the 'Giver of the Torah' through the medium of Torah. After the Beis haMikdash and the Land of Israel was destroyed, when the Nation of Israel was exiled, a major question arose, reflected in the words of the prophet, "*Why* has the land been laid to waste?" (*Yirmiyahu*, 9:11). Certainly, everyone knew that we were exiled as a result of our sins, but the question remained, 'What was the fundamental sin behind the spiritual collapse that led to this devastation?' The wise men, prophets, and the ministering angels were all asked this question and did not know how to answer, until Hashem explained, "Because they abandoned My Torah which I had given them" (*Yirmiyahu*, 9:12). This means, they abandoned 'My' Torah; they learned Torah, but did not recite the blessings on the Torah before engaging in its study (*Nedarim*, 81a).

Making a blessing on something means recognizing the Source of that thing. We recite a blessing over an apple to officially give thanks to the Creator of life Who created the apple and is allowing us to partake of it. Learning Torah without reciting a blessing over it means forgetting the 'Who' behind the Torah, the *Nosein haTorah* / One giving the Torah (The *Ran*, ad loc). There is a type of 'study' that is merely for the sake of gaining knowledge; it does not include an understanding that the Torah is *Divine* wisdom and a medium through which we connect to the Source of all life.

On a deeper level, to recite a blessing over learning Torah is not merely to remember Its Source, but to actually make a connection between the 'below' and the 'Above.' A Berachah connects the *Limud haTorah* / learning of the Torah with the *Nosen haTorah* / Giver of the Torah, as the Maharal explains (Hakdamah, *Tiferes Yisrael*. This idea is already stated in the Rishonim. See *Teshuvas haRashba*, Part 5: Siman, 51. *Sefer haChinuch*, Mitzvah 430 [Birchas HaMazon]. See also *Nefesh haChayim*, Sha'ar 2:2-3).

Rav Yoel Sirkis (1561-1640 CE), known as the Bach, wonders at why a seemingly light misdeed, omitting blessings before learning Torah (even though it may be a Torah-based Mitzvah), deserved such a harsh punishment (*Bach*, Orach Chayim, 47). He explains that when the prophet Yirmiyahu says, "because they abandoned My Torah which I had given them," it meant that in those times many were engaged in studying Torah, but it was for their own personal benefit. They merely wanted to know the laws of financial transactions to proudly show off their wisdom. Their intention was not to cleave to the holiness and spirituality of Torah which draws down Hashem's Presence into the world. By ignoring Hashem's Presence in the Torah, they actually caused a separation between Hashem's revealed Presence and the world. It therefore retreated and ascended.

"The Land has been laid to waste" means that the Divine Presence has departed from being revealed in this world. As these students were the cause of the exile of the Divine Presence, they too experienced an exile from their land.

These powerful words of the Bach are essential to our understanding of our relationship with the Torah, our intrinsic relation to the sacredness and Divinity of the Torah. They reveal to us how through learning Torah with *Deveikus* / fusion with Divinity, we draw the revealed Presence of Hashem into this world.

On this subject, here are the golden words of the Alter Rebbe (*Orach Chayim*, 47:1), "One must be most vigilant with regard to the blessings before studying Torah. Indeed, the Land [of Israel] was laid waste only because they did not recite the blessings that precede Torah. They did not hold the Torah in sufficient esteem to warrant the recitation of a blessing, and thus took its blessings lightly... Hashem's precious vessel, in which Hashem takes delight every day, should therefore be valued so highly by every individual that he recites its blessings with a joy that surpasses his joy over all the pleasures in the world. This shows that he engages in Torah *Lishmah* / for its own sake...."

When Torah is pondered simply as another intellectual subject, as another philosophical mental activity, what is then needed most is the left brain, to comprehend, analyze, assess, decipher. But, as they were approaching Mount Sinai they knew that the Torah is the Torah of Hashem; and through the Infinite Torah they're connecting to the Ein Sof, the pristine open space of the 'white fire' from where the 'black fire' arises. They surmised that sleep, dream, relative inward transcendence, *Ayin* / emptiness, and the emptying of their conscious rational selves, would be the most apt posture to receive the Torah.

BEYOND YESH & AYIN AND THE UNITY BETWEEN AWAKE/YESH AND ASLEEP/AYIN

Their error was in thinking that spirituality is closer to Hashem than physicality, that a dream-state is closer to the Divine than a normative awake state. Klal Yisrael assumed that to connect to the Ein Sof they needed to lessen their sense of Yesh, existence and rational selves in order to enter a more Ayin-like state. Yet, Hashem is the Creator of both body and soul, physical and spiritual, dream state and waking state, Yesh and Ayin. Nothing is closer or further to the Creator, as Hashem creates all; everything is ultimately a manifestation of Divine revelation and nothing more.

In this way, through the gift of the Torah we become more G-*dly*, not merely more 'spiritual,' as spirituality is simply the opposite side of physicality, and just another creation of the Creator. Through the Torah we can come to experience Deveikus with Hashem, the Creator of all life and expressions, without need for special spiritual states of consciousness.

And so, rather than going to sleep and receiving the Torah in an Ayin or dream-like state, we stay awake and receive the Torah in our waking Yesh state. On the other hand, if we were merely awake in the mundane sense, operating mostly from our rational mind, we might not be open to receive the Keser of Torah, the white fire of the Torah. Just as we do not exclusively connect with Hashem through Ayin, neither do we connect exclusively through Yesh. So to show that Hashem is beyond the polarities of transcendent and immanent, physical and spiritual, Ayin and Yesh, when we actually receive the Torah on Shavuos morning, our practice is to be in a 'combination' of both awake and asleep states simultaneously. Medical science calls this a 'hypnagogic' state, and Chazal define it as, "asleep but not asleep, awake but not awake" / נים ולא נים תיר ולא תיר (*Ta'anis*, 12b).

Following a full night of reciting the Tikun and learning Torah, most people are sleepy, maybe a little dreamy, and the borders of the individual self have faded; this is a subtle state of *Bitul* or Ayin. At the same time, we are vertical and awake and have at least some access to our rational mind, our physicality, our Yesh. In this way, we are both awake and asleep, and we can connect to the fullness of the Torah — both the white fire and the black fire. We can appreciate how the white fire is expressed through the black fire, and how the black merges back into the white, and ultimately, how they are equal unified expressions of Hashem Alone.

It is interesting to note that one of the earliest sources which speaks about the practice of staying up all night and learning is from Rav Yoseph Caro and Rav Shelomo Alkabetz. Rav Alkabetz described the events that occurred on a Shavuos night in a letter printed as the introduction to the book *Maggid Meisharim* by Rav Yoseph Caro. In the book he recorded many of the revelations that a *Maggid* / the angelic superconscious voice of the Mishnah (the "white fire" of the Mishnah) imparted to him. The letter describes the very first time Rav Yospeh Caro received this form of revelation, late that Shavuos night (Hakdamah, *Maggid Meisharim. Shaloh, Shavuos*, 29b-30a).

Writing a few years later, Rav Chayim Vital speaks about the mystical practice of tuning into the Maggid of the Mishnah (which is beyond the scope of this text), and, after delineating the method, he writes, "If you are not yet worthy or refined to receive this level, then because of the continuous movement of your mouth (in rapid recital of selected passages of the Mishnah), you will become tired and silent, and then you will start falling asleep, a condition of נים ולא נים, then in this semi-conscious state…" (*Sha'arei Kedushah*, 4:1,1). Thus, this state of נים ולא נים is connected to a type of revelation, and specifically to the night of Shavuos. The 'white fire' is being "asleep" and is the source of the revelation; whereas the 'black fire' is being "awake" and is the words of Torah that are revealed to us and through us, when early on Shavuos morning, we experience this unity of opposites.

DAIRY/AYIN, MEAT/YESH; ON SHAVUOS WE EAT BOTH

This perhaps is the deeper reason why on Shavuos the custom is to eat both meat, as on every other Yom Tov, and also dairy. Meat represents Yesh, fullness, and coarse physical existence. Dairy, by contrast, represents Ayin, emptiness and ethereal spirituality. On Shavuos we ingest and identify with both.

In the desert, Klal Yisrael asked Moshe for meat: "Who will give us flesh to eat?" (*Bamidbar*, 11:4). Moshe retorts, "From where can I produce meat?" / *me'Ayin Li Basar* / מאין לי בשר (*Ibid*, 13). Moshe, who took them out of Egypt and performed Hashem's marvelous miracles in Egypt as well as at the splitting of the sea, cannot produce meat? Why not? What Moshe is really saying is, "I am *Ayin*, so how can meat (desire) come from me?" I apparently cannot be the medium to draw down meat for Klal Yisrael, because I am Ayin, and meat is Yesh; Ayin cannot project Yesh. Moshe is saying, I can be the conduit to split the Yesh of the sea, or break the Yesh of Egyptians, but not, seemingly, to produce the Yesh of meat, the fullness of flesh and all it represents.

Moshe is *Ayin*. The humblest of men, 'empty' of all Yesh and ego. Even his name hints to Ayin. The three letters in Moshe's name are Mem, Shin, Hei. When these letters are spelled out, *Mem* is spelled Mem-Mem; *Shin* is spelled Shin, Yud, Nun; *Hei* is spelled Hei-Aleph. In *Mem* the additional letter when 'filled' is Mem. In *Shin* the added filling letters are Yud and Nun. In *Hei* the filling letter is *Aleph*. All of these filling letters together, Mem, Yud, Nun and Aleph can be arranged to spell the word *Me'ayin* / from Ayin, as Moshe is Ayin (Rav Menachem *Tziyoni*, v'Zos haBeracha. See also *Shaloh*, Shemos, 2).

Moshe is Ayin and therefore related to dairy, a more subtle and gentle nurturing product. Moshe feels that he is 'a nursemaid carrying a suckling child' (*Bamidbar*, 11:12. This verse is a statement, not a question. *Ohr haChayim*, ad loc). After the Exodus from Egypt, we were all like infants nursing from the 'bosom' of Hashem via the 'nursemaid' Moshe. We were in a state of *Yenikah* / suckling during our journey through the desert (*Sha'ar haKavanos, Derush Pesach*, 1). Thus, when others of Klal Yisrael prophesied in the desert, they too had names related to 'bosom,' such as in *El-Dad* / "to the bosom", and *Meydad* / "from the bosom" (See *Mishnas Chassidim, haChalav*, 1:1. There are right / *Chesed* and left / *Gevurah* sides of the bosom. In general, Moshe became the great transmitter of Torah because of the purity of his own 'nursing' (*Sotah*, 12b. Maharsha, ad loc).).

For this reason the *Mon* / Manna manifested in the merit of Moshe (*Ta'anis*, 9a). Mon, which appeared as a somewhat nondescript white seed, tasted like whatever food the eater wished. "And the taste of it was like the taste of a cake baked with oil" (*Bamidbar*, 11:8). Rav Avuha said, "Do not read *L'shad* / cake, but *Shad* / bosom. Just as an infant finds many flavors in the breast, so did *Klal Yisrael* find many tastes in the *Mon*" (*Yuma*, 75a). Mon is similar to mother's milk, and Moshe is the conduit to bring down this form of nurturing.

On the day Moshe received the Torah from Mount Sinai, we connected especially to dairy foods. However, as we are connecting to the level of Keser, beyond the binary realms of Ayin and Yesh, we celebrate the Yom Tov by eating both forms of food. (Although obviously not simultaneously, as combining these foods is impermissible by Halachah. However, as a single 'vessel' cannot always hold two opposite 'lights,' sometimes the way to receive the paradoxes of Keser is to internalize one of the opposites and then the other. In this case, one must wait six hours (time for another meal) to eat dairy after completing the eating of meat. After eating dairy, before eating meat, you should cleanse your palate with something *Pareve* / neither meat nor dairy, such as bread. Then rinse your mouth or drink a beverage, and wash your hands. In addition, many have the custom of waiting a certain period of time, such as an hour, before eating meat. After eating certain hard cheeses, a six-hour waiting period is required before eating meat.)

WHY SO MANY CUSTOMS ON SHAVUOS?

As we mentioned in Essay 4, today, while we are not bringing offerings in the Beis haMikdash, there is very little Torah and even Rabbinic law that is unique to this holiday. On the other hand, there are plenty of *Minhagim* / customs, such as staying up all night learning, eating dairy foods and placing vegetation in the Shul.

Minhagim express the ultimate unity between the Above and the below. *Torah she-b'Kesav* / the Written revealed Torah comes to us from Above, and we merely make ourselves into an empty vessel to receive the transmission. *Torah she-b'al-Peh* / the Oral Teaching is the development of Torah through the prism of human minds and hearts 'below,' as "Torah is not in Heaven" (*Devarim*, 30:12), and the Sages are given the privilege to make rulings according to human understanding.

Minhagim, however, are an even deeper expression of the light 'below.' While everything in Torah she-b'al-Peh is alluded to somewhere in Torah she-b'Kesav, Minhagim come more directly from our dedication and love, our desire to do something extra to connect with Hashem.

We perform Minhagim not because the Torah asks us or requires us to do so, nor even because the Sages advise or teach us to do so. In fact, it is a Mitzvah of the Torah to 'listen to the words of the Sages,' (*Devarim* 17:11, *Devarim* 32:7) and this is the reason, when performing a Mitzvah from our Sages, we can recite a blessing, "Blessed are You... Who sanctifies us... and *commanded* us..." (*Shabbos*, 23a). Because of the Torah's commandment to listen to the Sages, we affirm that *Hashem* is the One Who has commanded us to do that Mitzvah, as if the act were an explicit directive in the text of the Torah.

The light from below rises to such a degree that we can even assert, "the Minhag of our ancestors *is* Torah" (*Tosefos*, Menachos 20b). In other words, even though it is 'merely' a custom, it 'became' Torah. In fact, it is even possible, in certain instances, to recite a blessing on a universally practiced Minhag, saying, "Blessed are You... Who sanctifies us... and commanded us...." For instance, there is a Minhag, not mentioned by our Sages in the Gemara, to light the Menorah on Chanukah in *Shul* / synagogue and do so with a blessing (*Shulchan Aruch*, Orach Chayim 671:7, this is based on the opinion of many Rishonim (see Beis Yoseph, *Orach Chayim*, 671). Others argue that a blessing should not be recited (Teshuvas *Chacham Tzvi*, 88, Maharam Schick, *Yoreh De'ah*, 347). There is a custom to recite Half-Hallel on Rosh Chodesh, and there is a debate among the Rishonim if a blessing should be recited. For example, the *Rambam* and *Rashi* hold that no blessing should be recited. The *Rif* (*Shabbos*, 24b), *Rabbeinu Tam* (*Tosefos*, Ta'anis, 28b. *Tosefos*, Erechin, 10b), the *Tur* in name of the Rosh (*Tur*, *Orach Chayim*, 422), and the *Ran*, however, maintain that we do make blessings over important customs (See

Shulchan Aruch, Orach Chayim, 422:2).). Such a Minhag is a manifestation of Torah-consciousness in the lower realm, arising within the collective consciousness of Klal Yisrael, and demonstrating total unison with the Above.

Shavuos is filled with Minhagim. The inner idea of Minhagim, which is the Keser that maintains and is the root of everything and thus unifies all expressions of Above and below, is also the general theme of the entire month. It is the month of the 'twins,' the marriage of Heaven and earth, the joining of spiritual and physical, which is the posture of Matan Torah. The Medrash says, "Once there was a king who decreed, 'The people of Rome are forbidden to go down to Syria, and the people of Syria are forbidden to go up to Rome.' Similarly, when Hashem created the world He decreed, 'The Heavens are to Hashem (Above) and the earth (below) is given to man.' Yet, when Hashem desired to give the Torah, the original decree was rescinded and Hashem declared, 'The lower realms may ascend to the higher realms, and the higher realms may descend to the lower realms. And I, Myself, will begin' — as it is written, 'And *Hashem* descended on Mount Sinai'" (*Tanchumah*, Va'eira 15. *Medrash Rabbah*, Shemos 12:4).

Just as Hashem is revealed below, the below reveals Hashem. Through our counting 49 days to the day of Shavuos and refining our lives, we, 'the below' are participating in 'creating' Shavuos, as it were. And yet, on the 50th day, the Keser, the Divine Presence, comes down from Above on its own.

☾

Essay Eight
༜
SHAVUOS:
Beyond all Avodah

NOW, WHEN WE DO NOT BRING ANY SPECIAL OF-
FERING in the Beis haMikdash, we have no special
Mitzvos to perform on Shavuos. Even during the
times of the Beis haMikdash, when specific offerings were brought,
there was no unique focal item for the Yom Tov of Shavuos, such as
Matzah on Pesach, Lulav on Sukkos or Shofar on Rosh Hashanah.
Why is Shavuos different?

Many have asked this self-evident question (*Kedushas Levi*, Naso.
Tiferes Shelomo, Likutim, Derush Matan Torah). There are many unique and
interesting *Minhagim* / customs on Shavuos, such as eating dairy
foods, staying up all night, placing trees or grasses in Shul — but
none of these are Torah-based or even Rabbinic/Talmudic-based
practices, rather they are all Minhagim.

One way to address this question is the following. The Torah is infinitely transcendent, beyond the world of time and space (even though it simultaneously permeates time and space and is the blueprint of Creation or the template for time and space). Therefore, there is no human action, nor even Mitzvah, that can make us open to receive the infinitely transcendent Torah. On the contrary, to receive at this level we can only cease doing.

Actions exist in the realm of duality and finitude, *Alma d'Piruda* / the world of separation. Doing implies distinctions. In the matter of *doing*, each person is different, for each individual has their own idiosyncratic manner of doing things and each has different skills and aptitudes. By contrast, in the matter of *non-doing*, everyone is equal. Two people who are drawing pictures usually have very different looking results. The work of the one who has a fine arts degree is very different from that of the one who lacks any training and experience. However, when both refrain from drawing, their identical blank pieces of paper cannot be distinguished one from another. In this way, 'not doing' belongs to a world beyond distinctions, a world of infinity and unity.

If 'doing' expresses our finite selves, our individuality, our uniqueness, refraining from action reveals our deeper, infinite, unified self.

In the Mishnah, and later in the Gemara, Shavuos is called עצרת / *Atzeres* (*Mishnah Sheviit* 2:1, *Chagigah* 2:4, *Menachos* 3:6. From Rashi (if in fact it is Rashi's commentary on *Ta'anis*) it appears that in Tanach the Navi refers to Shavuos as *Atzeres*, "...קדשו צום קראו עצרה אספו זקנים כעצרת,(יואל א, יד),אמר קרא מה עצרת Rashi writes "מה עצרת - שבועות ושמיני עצרת" (Rashi, *Ta'anis*, 12b).). The word עצרת / *Atzeres* is related to the word *l'Atzor* / לעצור / to stop, to hold back. *Atzeres*, thus, means *to not do*. This holding back and ceasing from doing is also a type of nullification of the expressed ego (See *Zohar* 3, 97b). On Shavuos we stop; we temporarily cease from self-expression and from identifying as a separate individual.

For 49 days we counted and did the *Avodah* / spiritual-mental-emotional work of preparing ourselves, cleansing ourselves, ensuring that our *Midos* / interpersonal and inner traits are refined; but once we reach the 'foot of the mountain' and Matan Torah is about to occur, we need to stop. At that point we have arrived and just need to make ourselves into proper vessels to receive. We need to empty ourselves of our ego, our finite selves, our Yesh, as it were, and just receive. (Nonetheless, in the activity of 'Minhag' we *do* need to include and express the level of Yesh, as explored earlier.)

Not only are there no specific Shavuos Mitzvos or Mitzvah items in our days, the original Shavuos was mostly related to non-doing as well. For the experience of Matan Torah to be absorbed and integrated, and not merely a fleeting ecstatic experience, Hashem *did* give certain Mitzvos at the mountain. Inspiration is like a flame that must have a wick and oil to continue burning, and Mitzvos here ensure that the intense feelings of inspiration aroused at the Giving of the Torah would be anchored and concretized (*Kedushas Levi*, Naso). Yet, unlike other Yomim Tovim, the Mitzvos that Hashem gave us for that purpose were specifically acts of refraining, of *not doing*, of *l'Atzor* / לעצור holding back: to refrain from spousal relations, to stay off the mountain, and to refrain from touching the mountain.

Atzeres also means 'gather' and 'unify' (*Zohar* 3, 96b). Shavuos is a one day holiday, alluding to the Oneness of Hashem. It is a day that unifies all as one, since in non-doing we are all equal and unified.

Shavuos is also a day beyond nature, a day of infinity, of ceasing finite 'doing'; we are unified beyond our individual activities, talents, feelings or unique expressions of intelligence and identity.

When we refrain from certain actions, especially when we have a great desire to do them — such as going beyond the boundary and ascending the mountain upon which the Torah is being given — it demands 'infinite' self-control (See *Shem miShemuel*, Shavuos 5671). At Matan Torah Klal Yisrael successfully refrained from doing the three proscribed activities, and thus they deeply unified with each other and with themselves. They revealed their 'infinite' inner strength, and were able to become a true *Kli* / vessel to receive the infinite Torah, which is, "Longer than the earth's measure and wider than the sea" / ארכה מארץ מדה ורחבה מני־ים (*Iyov*, 11:9). Beyond מדה / measurement, which is 49 in numerical value, there is connection to the infinite ים, which is 50 in numerical value. That is, by ceasing from doing, there is made the space within to become one with the Infinite Giver of the Torah.

Essay Nine
႟

THE EVOLUTION OF KLAL YISRAEL:

From Am / People,
to Eidah / Congregation,
to Goy Echad / One Nation

IN ENGLISH, WHEN YOU REFER TO A LARGE GROUP OF PEOPLE from the same geographical location and who share a common culture you call them a nation or a people. In Torah vernacular, the children of Israel, the descendants of Yaakov, are referred to as an *Am*, as in, *Am Kadosh* / a holy people or *Am Yisrael* / the People of Israel, *Eidah* or *Adas* (plural of Eidah) Yisrael, and *Goy*, as in *Goy Kadosh* / a holy nation, or *Goy Echad* / a singular nation.

Am has been translated as *people*, *Eidah* is often rendered as *congregation*, and *Goy* is commonly interpreted as *nation*. It is axiomatic that the terms employed in Torah are precise. Yet, before exploring the nature of these three terms, it is important to understand what constitutes, and what creates, a nation.

In our times, old defined borders are breaking down and backlashes against nationalism are on the rise. At the same time, it seems every ethnic group aspires for their own homeland and sovereignty. The question arises: how does the Torah define 'a people'? From a colloquial way of understanding perhaps it is language or dialect that creates a people. Yet many nations around the world share a language, and yet are diametrically opposed to each other in terms such as government or culture. Perhaps then culture comprises 'a people.' But what is culture? Is it a group's 'high culture,' such as their shared value for certain fine arts or refined music? However in many countries around the world, such aesthetic and cultural values are shared by a very small subgroup. Maybe then it is the 'plebeian' culture that unites 'a people.' For example, in America, the 'fast food nation' culture has many common elements such as consuming large quantities of fast food, driving certain types of cars and rooting for sports teams. But, suppose one does not enjoy fast food, does not own a car, and is not a sports fan, would this person be considered less of an American or un-patriotic?

So what really binds a people as a nation? Perhaps a nation is formed by something rather coincidental, such as a common geographical location. On the other hand, the laws of citizenship, for example, apply to even those born abroad to American parents.

With these questions in mind, let us now drop into a deeper level and come to understand what is most important with regards to Shavuos; what makes Klal Yisrael 'a people'?

BIRTH OF KLAL YISRAEL

The going out of Egypt was the birth of Klal Yisrael, like a child being pulled out of the womb (*Medrash Tehilim*, 114:6). The entire unfolding of the ten *Makos* / plagues is similar to the

contractions of childbirth (*Likkutei Torah* (Arizal), Shemos, p 121). The very first action that Klal Yisrael was asked to perform while still slaves in Egypt was to bring the *Korban Pesach* / Paschal Lamb, and it was sacrificed immediately preceding the Exodus. In order to eat of it, the offering needed to be roasted over a spit with, "its heads upon its legs" (*Shemos*, 12:9). Its head upon its legs, as the Tzemech Tzedek explains (*Derech Mitzvosechah*, Korban Pesach. *Taamei haMitzvos* (Arizal), Bo), is the position of a fetus in the womb (*Nidah*, 30b). This teaches us that while we were still in Egypt we were in a condition like that of *Ibbur* / a fetus in its mother's womb (*Sha'ar haKavanos*, (Arizal) *Derushei Pesach* 1) and the going out of Egypt was our birth.

All the sufferings of enslavement in Egypt were the labor pains, and the Exodus was the birth. So let us observe the language which the Torah employs when discussing this birth and see if we can unearth a pattern that speaks of our evolution into a people.

Prior to the Exodus, when Moshe is first being appointed as the redeemer of Klal Yisrael, the Torah says, "And Hashem said, 'I have surely seen the affliction of עַמִּי / *My people* who are in Egypt, and have heard their cry because of their taskmasters, for I know their pains'" (*Shemos*, 3:7). The precise phrase the Torah uses is עַמִּי / *Ami* / My People. Hashem is telling Moshe about the plight of 'My *Am*' and letting Moshe know that he was chosen to help take Klal Yisrael out of affliction and enslavement.

Reluctantly, Moshe accepts his role. As the narrative unfolds, and as Klal Yisrael is still in Egypt, they receive the Mitzvah of *Korban Pesach*, the Divine command or invitation to offer a Paschal lamb. Introducing this Mitzvah the Torah says, "Speak to עדת / *Adas* / all the congregation of Israel, saying, 'on the tenth day of this month, let each one take a lamb for each parental home, a lamb for each household" (*Shemos*, 12:3). The title the Torah uses at this point for Klal Yisrael is עדת / *Adas*, the possessive form of the word *Eidah* / congregation.

Following the Exodus, as Klal Yisrael is standing at the foot of Mount Sinai, the Torah speaks once more, "And now, if you will obey My voice, and keep My covenant, then you shall be My own treasure among all peoples; for all the earth is Mine. And you shall be to Me a kingdom of priests and a holy גוי / *Goy*..." (*Shemos*, 19:5-6). The description used in this third statement is גוי / *Goy* / nation. This *Goy* categorization is apparently the apex of titles that Klal Yisrael receives at Matan Torah. "The beginning is wedged in the end" — at the very beginning of Klal Yisrael's collective journey, when our forefather Avraham first encountered Hashem he was told, "And I will make you into a great *Goy*" (*Bereishis*, 12:2). The message of the objective was clearly defined: the metamorphosis of his descendants into a great Goy, which was eventually achieved when they stood at Mount Sinai, receiving the Torah.

FROM AM TO EIDAH TO GOY

Three evolving stages are now evident. In the first stage, Klal Yisrael is referred to as an *Am*. This is the definition of Klal Yisrael before receiving any Mitzvos, a pre-Mitzvos 'people.' As an Am,

Klal Yisrael is afflicted with suffering and is in an ontological condition of exile.

Am is the definition of a people in its weakest state. In fact, the word *Am* means *almost extinguished*, as in *Gechalim* **Omemus** / barely lit, nearly extinguished coals (Rashi, *Pesachim*, 27a. Rashi, *Pesachim*, 75b. *Berachos*, 53b). The phrase עמי קלה means 'weak' (Rashi, *Chulin*, 38a). When the Torah or its commentary uses the term *Am*, we are to understand that this refers to a people in a weak state (*Sha'ar haYichud v'haEmunah*, 6).

In the pre-Mitzvos and pre-Torah reality, in a situation where there were little distinct separations, what forced a level of unity among Klal Yisrael was their common enemy. Being communally oppressed in Egypt, the external predicament pressed Klal Yisrael together into a more unified group. Indeed, historically, there are nations and peoples that coalesce as one group solely because of outside oppression or persecution. Take away all the outside influences, and the internal structure or unity of a people falls apart.

When Hashem speaks to Moshe about the suffering of Klal Yisrael, the term *Am* is used. Hashem says, "I have surely seen the affliction of My 'people' who are in Egypt, and have heard their cry because of their taskmasters, for I know their pains." Perhaps, these two statements are linked with each other. They are called an *Am* because of the affliction; the oppression creates the unity of the Am.

In the second stage, Klal Yisrael is referred to as *Eidah* / an assemblage of people. *Eidah* comes from the root word *Aid* / witness, a 'giver of testimony' or 'living testimony.'

An Eidah is a group of people beyond geographical circumstances that are unified by abiding laws and shared customs. Klal Yisrael becomes an Eidah when their lives become a testimonial to a higher order, to Hashem's Law. The higher definition of Klal Yisrael is that we are a people who are bound to the Torah and give testimony to Hashem's Presence in this world. Our lives are a living testimony to Hashem's sovereignty, to Hashem's Torah given to us to perfect Hashem's world. In the words of Rav Sadiyah Gaon, the Tenth Century philosopher, "The nation is only a nation with the Torah" / לפי שאומתינו בני ישראל אינה אומה אלא בתורותיה (*Emunos vDe'os*, Ma'amar 3:7). Upon receiving the Mitzvah of Korban Pesach, we thus became a genuine people, an *Aid* / witness, and were collectively called an *Eidah*.

Any group, any Am, can be an Eidah if they live to give testimony, to witness to an ideal or certain belief. Even idol worshippers can be an Eidah, giving testimony to a belief in an idol, as a worshipper of Avodah Zara is also called a *witness*, "Those who form idols that are all empty, and their treasures are of no avail, and they are their witnesses" (*Yeshayahu*, 44:9). The holidays of Avodah Zarah are called 'witnesses' (According to Rav. *Yerushalmi*, Berachos, 8:6. *Avodah Zarah*, 2a). The act of idol worship gives a testimony — albeit a testament to vanity and emptiness.

Klal Yisrael are called Hashem's witnesses, "'You are עדי / My witnesses,' says Hashem, 'and My servant whom I chose'" (*Yeshayahu*, 43:10). Collectively and individually each and every one of us is a living testimony to Hashem's Presence in this world; and a living testimony to the presence of the Holy Torah that Hashem has given us at Matan Torah and continues to give us.

The term *Goy* is the root word of *G'viyah* / body, as in, "Nothing remains before my Lord, except גויתנו / our bodies..." (*Bereishis*, 47:18. See Malbim, *Yair Ohr*, 6. Although, he writes that Am is higher than Goy).

The third stage, and pinnacle definition of Klal Yisrael, is *Goy Echad* / Singular Nation. This occured when Klal Yisrael, as a group of individuals, divided into tribes. Which, paradoxically, revealed the deepest truth that we are one *Goy*, one body, with multiple tribes. Klal Yisrael are not *Goyim* in the plural (although see *Ramban*, Bereishis 16:6), as the term *Goyim* generally refers to the 'many nations' of the world to the exclusion of Klal Yisrael. *Goy*, singular, refers to Klal Yisrael; *Goyim*, plural, refers to the nations of the world (בעשו כתיב ביה שש שש נפשות... וביעקב שבעים נפש אלא עשו שהוא עובד לאלהות הרבה כתיב) ביה נפשות הרבה, אבל יעקב שהוא עובד לאלוה אחד כתיב בו נפש אחת / By Esav it says, "souls" (plural)... whereas by Yaakov it says, seventy "soul" (singular)... Because Esav worshipped many deities, it is written many souls, but for Yaakov, who worshipped one G-d, it is written "one soul" (*Medrash Rabbah*, Vayikra, 4:6).). *Goy Echad* is a title reserved for Klal Yisrael, as Klal Yisrael are really one unified body (When one part of Klal Yisrael is hurting, it is felt by all (*Medrash*, ibid). Klal Yisrael is like a *Guf Echad* / single body with one *Nefesh* / soul (*Mechilta*, Rashbi, Yisro, 19:6 See Maharal, *Nesivos Olam*, Nesivos haTochacha, 2) — especially once they went into the "One Land," Eretz Yisrael (Shu't *Avnei Nezer*, Yoreh De'ah, 126:4. Shu't *Tzefnas Paneach* 1, 143:2. Maharal, ibid, *Nesiv Hatzdekah*, 6).).

When speaking about the Mitzvah not to take revenge, our Sages use the analogy of one hand of a person doing something negative and the other hand slapping it for doing so (*Yerushalmi*, *Nedarim*, 9:4). Taking revenge is like hitting yourself, as you are one with the other. Klal Yisrael is actually a *Tzuras Adam* / form of a person. There are different parts of the body, and everyone of Klal

Yisrael has a unique individual function and purpose. Some people are more related to the head of the collective body, and they pursue intellectual endeavors; others are more connected to the heart, and their endeavors are more emotion-based; whereas others are connected to the hands, and are focussed on actions. Yet, all of Klal Yisrael is one body, and those who are sensitive enough feel this in their gut; when one limb of the body hurts, whether physically or spiritually, the entire body feels the pain (Klal Yisrael is likened to a sheep, similar to a sheep when one part of the body hurts the entire body hurts (*Medrash Rabbah*, Vayikra, 4:6).). In the language of the Ritva (the great Spanish Rabbi, Yom Tov Asevilli / from Seville, 1260s-1312):

כל ישראל ערבין זה לזה וכלם כגוף אחד

"All of Israel are responsible for each other,
and all of them are like one body."

(Ritva, *Rosh Hashanah*, 29a)

We really first experienced this posture of total unity at Matan Torah, when we came to the Mountain, "And Israel encamped there opposite the Mountain" / ויחן־שם ישראל נגד ההר (*Shemos*, 19:2). The Torah is speaking of all Klal Yisrael, and instead of using the plural, as in ויחנו,

the Torah says ויחן — singular. Say our Sages, the singular form denotes that we encamped near the Mountain, "כאיש אחד / *k'Ish Echad* / like one person, בלב אחד / *b'Lev Echad* / with one heart" (*Mechilta*, Rashi ad loc). At the foot of Mount Sinai it was revealed to us that we are like one person, one body, a *Goy Echad*.

Interestingly, a seemingly similar expression is said by our Sages with regards to the Egyptians. Having allowed Klal Yisrael to leave

Egypt, Pharaoh had a change of heart and decided to chase after Klal Yisrael. The verse says, "Pharaoh drew near, and the children of Israel lifted up their eyes, and behold! The Egyptians were נֹסֵעַ / advancing after them" (Shemos, 14:10). A large army of Egyptians were chasing Klal Yisrael, yet the Torah uses the singular word נֹסֵעַ. Says Rashi, this tells us that the Egyptians chased Klal Yisrael בלב אחד / *b'Lev Echad* / with one heart, כאיש אחד / *k'Ish Echad* / like one person.

While these statements seem similar, there is a subtle but acute difference between them. With regards to Klal Yisrael it says first *k'Ish Echad* / like one person, and then *b'Lev Echad* / with one heart; whereas with regards to the Egyptians it first says *b'Lev Echad* and then *k'Ish Echad*. This is because for the Egyptians it was their shared 'heart,' their shared emotion, their shared envy and hatred of Klal Yisrael that unified them. They shared a 'heart' and thus unified as an Ish Echad. With Klal Yisrael it is the exact opposite. It was not shared values or emotions that created the unity, rather, the other way around; they sensed they were k'Ish Echad, a Goy Echad, and due to this they were also unified on the level of their ambitions and desires — Lev Echad.

Having reached Mount Sinai, we revealed the deepest truth of who we are; Klal Yisrael is one unified self, a human unity that expresses Hashem's unity.

BEING PART OF KLAL YISRAEL DESPITE EXTERNALITIES

As above, *Am* refers to the weakest manifestation of Klal Yisrael, and for the most part, *Am* is a forced unity of a people created by a common enemy such as the Egyptians. Indeed, some modern thinkers would like to suggest that a Jew is only a Jew because of the anti-Jew, the anti-Semite. This is a weak definition of Klal Yisrael, and a superficial reading, as it completely omits the importance of our mission, Mitzvos and Minhagim, and certainly the Divinity of the Torah. Suppose a person among Klal Yisrael does not experience anti-Semitism, either because they live in peaceful times or because they choose to 'hide' their Jewish identity. Are they less Jewish? According to the Torah, certainly not. Even a Jewish person who does not identify himself as Jewish, because he or she was "lost among the nations," is still one hundred percent Jewish.

Now suppose there is a Jew who does not, as of yet, demonstrate an outward willingness or desire to be a living Eidah of Torah and Hashem's presence, or join in some way with Klal Yisrael's spiritual destiny and ambitions. This could happen because of ignorance or lack of proper education or understanding, and again, being "lost among the nations." However, even if they do not identify themselves as part of the nation, even if they do not recognize that they are a Jew, they *are* still Jewish according to the Torah.

Even adherence to Torah and its values cannot be the sole root of Jewish identity; as even those Jews who do not claim, as of yet, the vast spiritual wealth of Torah as their own, are still considered Jews. So what then makes a person a Jew?

The ultimate answer is, being part of the *Goy Echad* is what makes every Jewish person a Jew. Even if they are not influenced by external oppression or persecution, and even if they do not yet adhere to or relate to an identity based upon Torah and Mitzvos, they are nonetheless part of the one body, the Goy Echad that stood at Mount Sinai.

To be born to a Jewish mother is to be born into the Goy Echad, into the one body and one family. This means being born *chosen* by the Creator to be part of this glorious noble family, who are all descendants and children of Avraham, Sarah, Yitzchak, Rivka, Yaakov, Rachel, Leah, Bilhah and Zilpah. Klal Yisrael is called *Bnei Yisrael* / Children of Israel, the offspring of the patriarch Yaakov, who is also called *Yisrael* / Israel (Matrilineal Jewish lineage (*Yevamos*, 45a), according to some Rishonim, began at Matan Torah. According to the Ramban, however, it began with Avraham (*Ramban*, Vayikra, 24:10).). Clearly, this sense of family extends itself outward and embraces those who choose Judaism as converts, as they become part of the family, and they too are "Children of Avraham and Sarah" (Rebbe Yehuda rules (*Yerushalmi*, Bikurim, 1:4, unlike the Mishnah, *Bikurim*, 1:4) that a *Ger* / convert can bring Bikurim and say regarding the Land of Israel, that Hashem has, "sworn to our ancestors" (*Devarim*, 26:3), since Avraham was designated as "the father of all nations" (*Bereishis*, 17:5), and Avraham was the father of many converts during his times, and the father of all future converts. The Rambam rules like Rebbe Yehudah (Rambam, *Hilchos Bikurim*, 4:3. See also *Tosefos*, Baba Basra, 81a).).

Within the nucleus of a family there are always different types of children. The diversity within the family unit is part of its dynamism. In every family, some members are more obedient than others and some more resistant than others; some are more involved in the spiritual path than their parents, etc. — but they are all part of the family.

All of Klal Yisrael are part of the Goy Echad, eternal members of the One Family, whether fully and openly committed to Hashem and Torah or not yet, whether fully identified as Jewish or not yet.

Even those who do not yet notice their deep connection to Hashem and His Torah show a disproportionate drive for social justice, a passion for truth, and a yearning love for knowledge. Even those we might call 'secular' Jews show a strong desire for independence and a need to change the world for the better. All these traits, perhaps unknown to them, are part of the *Yerushah* / inheritance from our ancestors, are derived from the Torah, and are expressions of being part of the Goy Echad.

Ever since the patriarchs (Avraham, Yitzchak and Yaakov) and the matriarchs (Sarah, Rivka, Rachel and Leah) walked this earth, relentlessly challenging their polytheistic and morally corrupt surroundings, and with self-abnegation pursued justice as well as taught and inspired monotheism, and thus accountability and responsibility, these traits have penetrated the very fiber of their 'family.' As each of these ancestors transformed themselves into luminaries and archetypal figures, their faith penetrated the deepest consciousness of their followers and offspring. They have bequeathed to us, their children, an innate faith in the Creator as well as faith in the ability of humankind to spiritually evolve and establish Divine justice and peace.

Our Avodah on Shavuos is to think about what it means to be *Mekabel* / receivers of the Torah. On Pesach we were, and are, chosen and birthed as a People. On Shauvos we answer the question 'why' we were chosen. Therefore we need to ask, Why I am Jewish? What is the destiny and purpose of Klal Yisrael, and am I living up to this potential? Are we living up to being a "nation of priests"? As Rashi writes, to be a *Kohen* means *l'Shareis* / 'to serve' others and the Infinite One, and in this way show the world what it means to live in a higher/deeper way. To live up to this task as a holy People requires that we live our own personal lives in holiness and bear witness to the Truth of Hashem's Torah.

This calling is a tremendous challenge. The Medrash (Vayikra Rabba, 6:5) beautifully interprets the Pasuk, "And he was a witness, as he has either seen or known of the matter; but if he does not testify, then he will carry the punishment" / והוא עד או ראה או ידע אם־לוא יגיד ונשא עונו (Vayikra, 5:1).

והוא עד אלו ישראל: ואתם עדי

"And he is a witness": this refers to Klal Yisrael, as Hashem says regarding them, "You are My witness…"

או ראה: אתה הראת לדעת...,

"As he has seen": this refers again to Klal Yisrael, who saw at Mount Sinai the presence of Hashem.

או ידע: וידעת היום.

"Or has known the matter": This also refers to Klal Yisrael who know Hashem.

אם לא יגיד ונשא עונו, אם לא תגידו אלהותי לאמות העולם הרי אני פורע מכם...

"But if he does not testify,
then he will carry the punishment":
This means that if we do not testify to the peoples of the world regarding Hashem's presence, then we carry the punishment.

In other words, part of our task as Jews is to be a witness and living testimony of Hashem's revelation and presence in the world.

We need to continually bring to the world the great truths of the Torah, that man is created in the Divine image; that life is sacred and has hope, purpose, meaning, and higher values; that life progresses, that Redemption is possible, and that time is linear and moving forward toward this ultimate fruition.

If we do not bear witness to the Truth and help teach the world about the Existence of HaKadosh Baruch Hu, then the 'burden' is with us — the corruption of the world is partially our 'fault' as it were. The revelation of the Torah is not 'complete' until we let it flow through us to fill the world.

All of the great ideas that humanity pursues are actually rooted in the Torah. From faith in the goodness of reality, the possibility of a better future and an ability to progress, improve and renew ourselves in linear time, to the value of thinking, speaking and acting with deep responsibility. From celebrating human uniqueness and individuality, to unifying under an ideal of freedom, justice and wellbeing for all, the gems of Torah wisdom now glitter throughout the world.

Our collective goal and ambition, the relentless drive of the Goy Echad, is to reveal in this world the Presence of Hashem Echad, and to prepare ourselves and the world for *Geulah* / Redemption. Even 'secular' Jews — who have, as of now, less connection to the inner aspects of Torah and Deveikus — even if they don't know it, also yearn to be an instrument to draw the world into peace, in which, "there will be neither famine, war, envy, or even competition; for good will flow in abundance and all the delights will be freely available as dust. The occupation of the entire world will be solely to know Hashem" (Rambam, *Hilchos Melachim uMilchamoseihem*, 12:5).

Yisrael has five letters which, in numerical value, equal 541 (Yud/10, Shin/300, Reish/200, Aleph/1 and Lamed/30 = 541). This is the same value as the Hebrew words *Ohr* / Light *v'Choshech* / and darkness (*Ohr* = Aleph/1, Vav/6, Reish/200; *v'Choshech* = Vav/6, Ches/ 8, Shin/ 300, Chaf/20 = 541). Indeed, our collective goal and aspiration is to inspire a unity between light and darkness, in such a way that the darkness will be transformed into light. Thus, as a family, we will continue to be a "light unto the nations," bringing light where there is darkness, warmth where there is cold, and a ray of hope when despair threatens to overwhelm; until the time when, "death will be banished" and, "the world will be filled with the knowledge of Hashem as the waters cover the sea" (Rambam, *ibid*).

Then, the luminous seeds planted in the soil of human consciousness at Matan Torah, and on every Shavuos, will have come to their complete splendorous fruition; there will be an end to the world of chaos, darkness and confusion, and Hashem's Light, Presence and Oneness will be fully revealed.

Other Books by the Author

RECLAIMING THE SELF
The Way of Teshuvah

Teshuvah is one of the great gifts of life. It speaks of a hope for a better today and empowers us to choose a brighter tomorrow. But what exactly is Teshuvah? How does it work? How can we undo our past and how do we deal with guilt? And what is healthy regret without eroding our self-esteem? In this fascinating and empowering book, the path for genuine transformation and a way to include all of our past in the powerful moment of the now, is explored and demonstrated.

THE MYSTERY OF KADDISH
Understanding the Mourner's Kaddish

The Mystery of Kaddish is an in-depth exploration into the Mourner's Prayer. Throughout Jewish history, there have been many rites and rituals associated with loss and mourning, yet none have prevailed quite like the Mourner's Kaddish Prayer, which has become the definitive ritual of mourning. The book explores the source of this prayer and deconstructs the meaning to better understand the grieving process and how the Kaddish prayer supports and uplifts the bereaved through their own personal journey to healing.

UPSHERNISH: The First Haircut
Exploring the Laws, Customs & Meanings
of a Boy's First Haircut

What is the meaning of Upsherin, the traditional celebration of a boy's first haircut at the age of three? Why is a boy's hair allowed to grow freely for his first three years? What is the deeper import of hair in all its lengths and varieties? What is the meaning of hair coverings? Includes a guide to conducting an Upsherin ceremony.

A BOND FOR ETERNITY
Understanding the Bris Milah

What is the Bris Milah – the covenant of circumcision? What does it represent, symbolize and signify? This book provides an in depth and sensitive review of this fundamental Mitzvah. In this little masterpiece of wisdom – profound yet accessible —the deeper meaning of this essential rite of passage and its eternal link to the Jewish people, is revealed and explored.

REINCARNATION AND JUDAISM
The Journey of the Soul

A fascinating analysis of the concept of Gilgul / Reincarnation. Dipping into the fountain of ancient wisdom and modern understanding, this book addresses and answers such basic questions as: What is reincarnation? Why does it occur? And how does it affect us personally?

INNER RHYTHMS
The Kabbalah of MUSIC

Exploring the inner dimension of sound and music, and particularly, how music permeates all aspects of life. The topics range from Deveikus/Unity and Yichudim/Unifications, to the more personal issues, such as Simcha/Happiness and Marirus/ sadness.

MEDITATION AND JUDAISM
Exploring the Jewish Meditative Paths

A comprehensive work encompassing the entire spectrum of Jewish thought, from the sages of the Talmud and the early Kabbalists to the modern philosophers and Chassidic masters. This book is both a scholarly, in-depth study of meditative practices, and a practical, easy to follow guide for any person interested in meditating the Jewish way.

TOWARD THE INFINITE

A book focusing exclusively on the Chassidic approach to meditation known as Hisbonenus. Encompassing the entire meditative experience, it takes the reader on a comprehensive and engaging journey through this unique practice. The book explores the various states of consciousness that a person encounters in the course of the meditation, beginning at a level of extreme self-awareness and concluding with a state of total non-awareness.

THIRTY – TWO GATES OF WISDOM
into the Heart of Kabbalah & Chassidus

What is Kabbalah? And what are the differences between the theoretical, meditative, magical and personal Kabbalistic teachings? What are the four paths of interpreting the teachings of the ARIzal? What did Chassidus teach? These are some of the fundamental issues expanded upon in this text. And then, more specifically, why are there so many names of G-d and what do they represent? What are the key concepts of these deeper teachings?

The book explores the grand narrative of the great chain of reality, how there was and is a movement from the Infinite Oneness of Hashem to a world of (apparent) duality and multiplicity.

THE PURIM READER
The Holiday of Purim Explored

With a Persian name, a masquerade dress code and a woman as the heroine, Purim is certainly unusual amongst the Jewish holidays. Most people are very familiar with the costumes, Megilah and revelry, but are mystified by their significance. This book offers a glimpse into the hidden world of Purim, uncovering these mysteries and offering a deeper understanding of this unique holiday.

EIGHT LIGHTS
8 Meditations for Chanukah

What is the meaning and message of Chanukah? What is the spiritual significance of the Lights of the Menorah? What are the Lights telling us? What is the deeper dimension of the Dreidel? Rav Pinson, with his trademark deep learning and spiritual sensitivity guides us through eight meditations relating to the Lights of the Menorah, the eight days of Chanukah, and a fascinating exploration of the symbolism and structure of the Dreidel. Includes a detailed how-to guide for lighting the Chanukah Menorah.

THE IYYUN HAGADAH
An Introduction to the Haggadah

In this beautifully written introduction to Passover and the Haggadah, we are guided through the major themes of Passover and the Seder night. This slim text, addresses the important questions, such as: What is the big deal of Chametz? What are we trying to achieve through conducting a Seder? What's with all that stuff on the Seder Plate? And most importantly, how is this all related to freedom?

PASSPORT TO KABBALAH
A Journey of Inner Transformation

Life is a journey full of ups and downs, inside-outs, and unexpected detours. There are times when we think we know exactly where we want to be headed, and other times when we are so lost we don't even know where we are. This slim book provides readers with a passport of sorts to help them through any obstacles along their path of self-refinement, reflection, and self-transformation.

———

THE FOUR SPECIES
The Symbolism of the Lulav & Esrog

The Four Species have inspired countless commentaries and traditions and intrigued scholars and mystics alike. In this little masterpiece of wisdom both profound and practical - the deep symbolic roots and nature of the Four Species are explored. The Na'anuim, or ritual of the Lulav movement, is meticulously detailed and Kavanos,, are offered for use with the practice. Includes an illustrated guide to the Lulav Movements.

———

THE BOOK OF LIFE AFTER LIFE

What is a soul? What happens to us after we physically die?

What is consciousness, and can it survive without a physical brain?

Can we remember our past lives?

Do near-death experiences prove immortality?

What is Gan Eden? Resurrection?

Exploring the possibility of surviving death, the near-death experience and a glimpse into what awaits us after this life.

(This book is an updated and expanded version of the book; Jewish Wisdom of the Afterlife)

THE GARDEN OF PARADOX:
The Essence of Non - Dual Kabbalah

This book is a Primer on the Essential Philosophy of Kabbalah presented as a series of 3 conversations, revealing the mysteries of Creator, Creation and Consciousness. With three representational students, embodying respectively, the philosopher, the activist and the mystic, the book, tackles the larger questions of life. Who is G-d? Who am I? Why do I exist? What is my purpose in this life? Written in clear and concise prose, the text, gently guides the reader towards making sense of life's paradoxes and living meaningfully.

BREATHING & QUIETING THE MIND

Achieving a sense of self-mastery and inner freedom demands that we gain a measure of hegemony over our thoughts. We learn to choose out thoughts so that we are not at the mercy of whatever belches up to the mind. Through quieting the mind and conscious breathing we can slow the onrush of anxious, scattered thinking and come to a deeper awareness of the interconnectedness of all of life.

Source texts are included in translation, with how-to-guides for the various practices.

VISUALIZATION AND IMAGERY:
Harnessing the Power of our Mind's Eye

We assume that what we see with our eyes is absolute. Yet, beyond our ability to choose what we see, we have the ability to choose how we see. This directly translates into how we experience life. In a world saturated with visual imagery, our senses are continuously assaulted with Kelipa/empty/fantasy imagery that we would not necessarily choose. These images can negatively affect our relationship with ourselves, with the world around us, and with the Divine. This volume seeks to show us how we can alter that which we observe through harnessing the power of our mind's eye, the inner sanctum of our imagination. We thus create a new way to see and experience the world. This book teaches us how to utilize visualization and imagery as a way to develop our spiritual sensitivity and higher intuition, and ultimately achieve Deveikus/Unity with Hashem.

SOUND AND VIBRATION:
Tuning into the Echoes of Creation

Through our perception of sound and vibration we internalize the world around us. What we hear, and how we process that hearing, has a profound impact on how we experience life. What we hear can empower us or harm us. A defining human capacity is to harness the power sound -- through speech, dialogue, and song, and through listening to others. Hearing is primary dimension of our existence. In fact, as a fetus our ears were the first fully operating sensory organs to develop.

This book will guide you in methods of utilizing the power of sound and vibration to heal and maintain mental, emotional and spiritual health, to fine-tune your Midos and even to guide you into deeper levels of Deveikus / conscious unity with Hashem. The vibratory patterns of the Aleph-Beis are particularly useful portals into our deeper conscious selves. Through chanting and deep listening, we can use the letters and sounds to shift our very mindset, to induce us into a state of presence and spiritual elevation.

THE POWER OF CHOICE:
A Practical Guide to Conscious Living

It is the essential premise of this book that we hold the key to unlock many of the gates that seem closed to us and keep us from living our fullest life. That key we all hold is the power to choose. The Power of Choice is the primary tool that we have at our disposal to impact the world and effect change within our own lives. We often give up this power to outside forces such as the market, media, politicians or peer pressure; or to internal forces that often function beyond our conscious control such as ego, anger, lust, greed or jealousy. Making conscious, compassionate and creative decisions is the cornerstone of living a mature and meaningful life.

MYSTIC TALES FROM THE EMEK HAMELECH

Mystic Tales of the Emek HaMelech, is a wondrous and inspiring collection of stories culled from the Emek HaMelech. Emek HaMelech, from which these stories have been taken, (as well as its author) is a bit of a mystery. But like all good mysteries, it is one worth investigating. In this spirit the present volume is being offered to the general public in the merit and memory of its saintly author, as well as in the hopes of introducing a vital voice of deeper Torah teaching and tradition to a contemporary English speaking audience

INNER WORLDS OF JEWISH PRAYER
A Guide to Develop and Deepen the Prayer Experience

While much attention has been paid to the poetry, history, theology and contextual meaning of the prayers, the intention of this work is to provide a guide to finding meaning and effecting transformation through the prayer experience itself.

Explore: *What happens when we pray? *How do we enter the mind-state of prayer? *Learning to incorporate the body into the prayers. *Discover techniques to enhance and deepen prayer and make it a transformative experience.

This empowering and inspiring text, demonstrates how through proper mindset, preparation and dedication, the experience of prayer can be deeply transformative and ultimately, life-altering.

WRAPPED IN MAJESTY
Tefillin - Exploring the Mystery

Tefillin, the black boxes and leather straps that are worn during prayer, are curiously powerful and mysterious. Within the inky black boxes lie untold secrets. In this profound, passionate and thought-provoking text, the multi-dimensional perspectives of Tefillin are explored and revealed. Magically weaving together all levels of Torah including the Peshat (literal observation), to Remez (allegorical), to Derush, (homiletic), to Sod (hidden) into one beautiful tapestry. Inspirational and instructive, Wrapped in Majesty: Tefillin, will make putting on the Tefillin more meaningful and inspiring.

SECRETS OF THE MIKVAH:
Waters of Transformation

A Mikvah is a pool of water used for the purpose of ritual immersion; a place where one moves from a state of Tumah; impurity, blockage and death— to a place of Teharah; purity, fluidity and life.

In SECRETS OF THE MIKVAH, Rav Pinson delves into the transformative powers of the Mikvah with his trademark all-encompassing perspective that ranges from the literal, Pshat observation and Halachic implications of the texts, to the allegorical, the philosophical, and finally, to the deep secrets of the

Mikvah as revealed by Kabbalah and Chassidus.

This insightful and inspirational text demonstrates how immersion in a Mikvah can be a transformative and life-altering practice, and includes various Kavanos—deep intentions—for all people, through various stages of life, that empower and enrich the immersion experience.

THE SPIRAL OF TIME:
A 12 Part Series on the Months of the Year.
The following titles from the series are now available!

THE SPIRAL OF TIME:
Unraveling the Yearly Cycle

Many centuries ago, the Sages of Israel were the foremost authority in the fields of both astronomical calculation and astrological wisdom, including the deeper interpretations of the cycles and seasons. Over time, this wisdom became hidden within the esoteric teachings of the Torah, and as a result was known only to students and scholars of the deepest depths of the tradition. More recently, the great teachers, from R. Yitzchak Luria (the Arizal) to the Baal Shem Tov, taught that as the world approaches the Era of Redemption, it is a Mitzvah / spiritual obligation to broadly reveal this wisdom.

"The Spiral of Time" is volume 1 is a series of 12 books, and serves as an introductory book to the basic concepts and nature of the Hebrew calendar and explores the special day of Rosh Chodesh.

THE MONTH OF SHEVAT:
ELEVATING EATING
& The Holiday of Tu b'Shevat

Each month of the year radiates with a distinct Divine energy and thus unique opportunities for growth, *Tikkun* and illumination. According to the deeper teachings of the Torah, all of these distinct qualities, opportunities and natural phenomena correspond to a certain data set. That is, the nature of each month is elucidated by a specific letter of the Aleph Beis, a tribe, verse, human sense, and so forth. The month of Shevat is particularly connected to food and our relationship to bodily intake. During this month we celebrate Tu b'Shevat, the New Year of the Tree, and aspire to create a proper and physically/emotionally/spiritually healthy relationship with food.

THE MONTH OF ADAR:
Transformation Through Laughter & Holy Doubt

Each month of the year radiates with distinct Divine qualities and unique opportunities for growth and spiritual illumination. As Adar concludes the monthly cycle of the year, as well as the solar phenomena of the winter, it is an appropriate month to think about our essential identity, before moving out to meet the world come spring. This month we strive to create a healthy relationship with holy humor, unbounded joy, and a general sense of lightness of being. Through the work of Adar we transform negative, crippling doubt and uncertainties into radical wonderment and openness.

THE MONTH OF IYYAR:
EVOLVING THE SELF
& The Holiday of LAG B'OMER

The month of IYYAR is the second month of the spring, a month that connects the Redemption from Egypt in Nissan with the Revelation of Torah in Sivan. The Chai/ Eighteenth day of the Month is the day we celebrate the Rashbi (Rabbi Shimon Bar Yochai) and the revealing of the hidden aspects of the Torah. This is the 'Holiday' of Lag b'Omer. The book explores the unique quality of this special month, a month that has a Mitzvah of counting the Omer every day. In addition, the book explores the roots and significance of the mystical 'holiday' of Lag b'Omer. Including the customs & Practices of Lag b'Omer, such as, bonfires, bows & arrows, parades, Upsherin, and more.

THE MONTHS OF TAMUZ AND AV:
Embracing Brokenness –
17th of Tamuz, Tisha B'Av, & Tu B'Av

Each month and season of the year, radiates with distinct Divine qualities and unique opportunities for growth and Tikkun.

The summer month of Tamuz and Av contain the longest and hottest days of the year. The raised temperature is indicative of a corresponding spiritual heat, a time of harsher judgement and potential destruction, such as the destructions of the first and second Beis HaMikdash, which began on the 17th of Tamuz and culminated on the 9th and 10th of Av.

A few days later, on Tu b'Av, the darkness is transformed and reveals the greatest light and possibility for new life. During these summer months of Tamuz and Av we embrace our brokenness so that we can heal and transform darkness into light.

THE MONTH OF ELUL:
Days of Introspection and Transformation

Each month of the year radiates with a distinct quality and provides unique opportunities for growth and personal transformation. Elul, as the final month of the spring/summer season is connected to endings. Elul gives us the strength to be able to finish strong, to end well. Elul also serves as a month of preparation for the New Year/Rosh Hashanah.

We inhale our past year, ending with wisdom and then we also gain the wisdom to begin anew and exhale a positive year into being. The mental, emotional, and spiritual objective of this month is introspection and the reclaiming of our inner purity and wholeness.

THE MONTH OF CHESHVAN:
Navigating Transitions, Elevating the Fall

Directly on the heels of the inspiring and holiday-filled month of Tishrei, Cheshvan is a month that is quiet and devoid of holidays. In the month of Cheshvan we use the stored up energies of the previous months to self-generate our inspiration and creativity and provide ourselves with the strength to rise up after a fall. In Cheshvan we are entering into a stormier, wetter and colder season. It is a month of transition. The mental, emotional and spiritual objective of this month is to weather the transitions, learn to self-generate and stand tall. And if we do fall, we use the quality of this month to get back up and do so with more conviction, strength, wisdom and clarity.

THE MONTH OF TEVES:
Refining Relationships, Elevating the Body

The quality of Teves is generally harsh—much like its counterpart Tamuz in the summer, thus the tendency for many is to hunker down, retract, curl up and wait for the month to pass by, only to reemerge when the harshness has dissipated. Think for a moment about the 'easier' months of the year, which, like gentle waves in the ocean, carry us where we want to go. We can ride these energies easily and they can propel us forward effortlessly, we just need to go with the overall flow, so to speak. The harsher months, on the other hand, can be compared to the more powerful waves that emanate from the belly of the ocean, which come forcefully crashing down and can easily drown a person before they even realize what has happened. However, those who want to utilize the momentum of the powerful energy that is available during such times can, with caution and creativity, harness these intense waves and ride them higher and farther than other, more gentle circumstances may allow. However, harnessing the power of Tohu, the raw energy of the body, does in fact need to be approached with great care and attention.

----

www.ingramcontent.com/pod-product-compliance
Lightning Source LLC
Chambersburg PA
CBHW060756100426
42813CB00004B/833